21ST CENTURY READING

CREATIVE THINKING AND READING WITH TEDTALKS

2

Laurie Blass • Mari Vargo • Eunice Yeates

 NATIONAL GEOGRAPHIC LEARNING |  CENGAGE Learning

Australia • Brazil • Japan • Korea • Mexico • Singapore • Spain • United Kingdom • United States

21ˢᵗ Century Reading Student Book 2
Creative Thinking and Reading with
TED Talks

Laurie Blass

Mari Vargo

Eunice Yeates

Publisher: Andrew Robinson

Executive Editor: Sean Bermingham

Development Editor: Tom Jefferies

Editorial Assistant: Dylan Mitchell

Director of Global Marketing: Ian Martin

Product Marketing Manager: Anders Bylund

Media Researcher: Leila Hishmeh

Director of Content and Media Production:
Michael Burggren

Production Manager: Daisy Sosa

Senior Print Buyer: Mary Beth Hennebury

Cover and Interior Designers: Scott Baker
and Aaron Opie

Cover Image: Amy Cuddy: ©James Duncan
Davidson/TED

Composition: Cenveo® Publisher Services

Student Book
ISBN 13: 978-1-305-26570-7

National Geographic Learning/Cengage Learning
20 Channel Center Street
Boston, MA 02210
USA

Cengage Learning is a leading provider of customised learning solutions with office locations around the globe, including Singapore, the United Kingdom, Australia, Mexico, Brazil and Japan. Locate our local office at **international.cengage.com/global**

Cengage Learning products are represented in Canada by Nelson Education Ltd.

Visit National Geographic Learning online at **NGL.Cengage.com**
Visit our corporate website at **www.cengage.com**

Printed in the United States of America
Print Number: 02   Print Year: 2016

CONTENTS

SCOPE AND SEQUENCE

Unit/Theme	Lesson A Reading	Reading Skills	Critical Thinking
1 **STARTING UP** *Interdisciplinary*	*Inspired Leadership* Magazine-style article	• Getting the main ideas • Identifying supporting ideas • Understanding references • Getting meaning from context	• Reflecting on own experienc • Applying ideas to other contexts
2 **FRAGILE FORESTS** *Conservation*	*Trouble for the Air Plants* Scientific article	• Getting the main ideas • Understanding key details • Scanning for information • Getting meaning from context	• Reasoning solutions • Interpreting a writer's statement
3 **BRIGHT IDEAS** *Health / Innovations*	*Big Problems, Simple Solutions* Magazine-style article	• Getting the main ideas • Understanding key details • Understanding visuals • Making inferences • Getting meaning from context	• Evaluating and justifying an opinion
4 **GAME CHANGERS** *Sociology / Technology*	*Is Gaming Good for You?* Research report	• Getting the main ideas • Understanding key details • Analyzing pros and cons • Understanding data • Getting meaning from context	• Inferring reasons • Reflecting on own experienc
5 **LESSONS IN LEARNING** *Psychology / Education*	*Engaging Learners* Research report	• Getting the main ideas • Understanding key details • Supporting ideas with evidence • Finding similarities and differences • Getting meaning from context	• Reflecting on own experienc
6 **FOOD FOR LIFE** *Food / Health*	*Food Revolution* Magazine-style article	• Getting the main ideas • Identifying problems and solutions • Understanding infographics • Getting meaning from context	• Applying information • Reflecting on own experienc
7 **BODY SIGNS** *Behavior / Psychology*	*Power Poses* Research report	• Getting the main ideas and details • Recognizing text structure	• Analyzing statements • Reflecting on own experienc
8 **ENERGY BUILDERS** *Energy / Engineering*	*Kite Power* News report	• Getting the main ideas • Scanning for specific information • Making comparisons • Getting meaning from context	• Evaluating and justifying an opinion • Reflecting on possible solutions
9 **CHANGING PERSPECTIVES** *Engineering / Art*	*Thinking in Pictures* Biographical article	• Scanning for information • Getting the main ideas • Understanding key details • Getting meaning from context	• Inferring meaning in statements • Reflecting on possibilities
10 **DATA DETECTIVES** *Statistics / Economics*	*Information Is Beautiful* Magazine-style article	• Getting the main ideas • Understanding infographics • Getting meaning from context	• Inferring meaning in statements • Reflecting on own experienc

Lesson B	TED Talks	Academic Skills	Critical Thinking	Project
	How to Start a Movement Derek Sivers	• Understanding main ideas and key details • Identifying tone and attitude	• Reflecting on own experience • Synthesizing information	• Researching other movements
	Conserving the Canopy Nalini Nadkarni	• Understanding main ideas and key details • Recognizing purpose • Recognizing supporting evidence	• Inferring reasons • Synthesizing information	• Researching a sustainability project
	A Warm Embrace that Saves Lives Jane Chen	• Understanding main ideas and key details • Identifying solutions • Visualizing a process	• Predicting solutions • Synthesizing information • Interpreting a statement	• Researching low-cost innovations
	Gaming Can Make a Better World Jane McGonigal	• Understanding main ideas and key details • Summarizing • Recognizing tone and message	• Inferring statements • Reflecting on own experience • Evaluating information	• Creating a proposal for a new game
	The Key to Success? Grit Angela Lee Duckworth	• Understanding main ideas • Understanding overall message • Understanding terms • Summarizing the talk	• Predicting reasons • Synthesizing information • Reflecting on own experience	• Preparing a survey on success
	Teach Every Child About Food Jamie Oliver	• Understanding main ideas and key details	• Inferring meaning • Evaluating information • Reflecting on own experience	• Planning an event to promote Food Revolution Day
	Your Body Language Shapes Who You Are Amy Cuddy	• Understanding main ideas and key details • Recognizing sequence • Identifying purpose • Summarizing	• Reflecting on own experience • Inferring statements • Reasoning ideas	• Practicing power poses
	How I Harnessed the Wind William Kamkwamba	• Understanding main ideas • Visualizing a process • Understanding causes and effects	• Inferring meaning • Synthesizing information	• Researching solutions to energy problems
	Deep Sea Diving. . . in a Wheelchair Sue Austin	• Understanding main ideas and key details • Recognizing tone and message	• Inferring meaning • Comparing information	• Researching people who challenge our assumptions
	The Beauty of Data Visualization David McCandless	• Understanding main ideas and key details	• Analyzing information • Reflecting on own experience • Interpreting a speaker's statement	• Creating an infographic

WHAT IS 21ST CENTURY READING?

21ST CENTURY READING develops essential knowledge and skills for learners to succeed in today's global society. The series teaches core academic language skills and incorporates 21st century themes and skills such as global awareness, information literacy, and critical thinking.

Each unit of 21st Century Reading has three parts:

• **READ** about a 21st century topic—such as online gaming—in Lesson A.

• **LEARN** more about the topic by viewing an authentic TED Talk in Lesson B.

• **EXPLORE** the topic further by completing a collaborative research project.

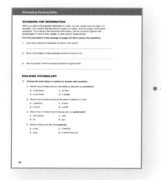

VOCABULARY BUILDING

READING SKILLS

LANGUAGE SKILLS

Strategies for understanding key ideas, language use, and purpose.

BUSINESS AND TECHNOLOGY

GLOBAL AWARENESS

21ST CENTURY THEMES

Interdisciplinary topics that affect everyone in a global society.

LEARNING SKILLS

The "4 Cs" that all learners need for success in a complex world.

CRITICAL THINKING AND COMMUNICATION

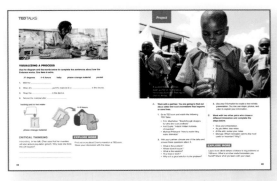

CREATIVITY AND COLLABORATION

21ST CENTURY LITERACIES

The ability to deal with information in a variety of modern formats and media.

VISUAL LITERACY

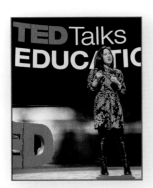

INFORMATION AND MEDIA LITERACIES

→ For more on 21st century learning, see **www.p21.org** and **21foundation.com.**

STARTING UP

GOALS

IN THIS UNIT, YOU WILL:

- Read about the characteristics of successful leaders.
- Learn about the role of followers.
- Explore how different movements start.

THINK AND DISCUSS

1. What do you think the people in the photo are doing? Read the caption to check.

2. What factors make a movement like Earth Hour successful?

Tunisians light candles during Earth Hour. Earth Hour encourages communities to turn off nonessential lights for one hour to raise awareness of environmental issues. The movement now engages over 7,000 cities and towns worldwide.

PRE-READING

A. Look at the title of the reading passage on page 11. What do you think makes a leader inspiring? List the four most important factors below. Then share your ideas with a partner.

1. _____

2. _____

3. _____

4. _____

B. Look at the picture of Dr. Martin Luther King Jr., and read the caption on this page. Why do you think he is considered a great leader? Discuss your ideas with a partner.

C. Look at the title and headings in the reading passage on pages 10–12. Read the first sentence in each paragraph. What do you think the passage is about?

_____

_____

_____

_____

In 1963, civil rights leader Martin Luther King Jr. gave his famous "I Have a Dream" speech to 250,000 people in Washington, D.C., U.S.A.

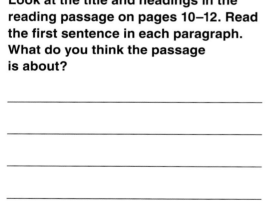

1 In the summer of 1963, 250,000 people **showed up** in Washington, D.C., to hear Martin Luther King Jr. speak. No emails were sent out, and there was no website to check the date. And yet thousands of people went. "How do you do that?" asks Simon Sinek.

INSPIRED LEADERSHIP

FOCUS ON BELIEFS

2 Sinek, an author and consultant who studies **leadership**, has a theory about why some leaders are able to inspire others to action. He thinks that great leaders, above all, **focus** on what they believe. They answer questions like "What's my **purpose**? Why does my organization exist? Why do I get out of bed in the morning?" For example, Martin Luther King Jr. **stood out** as a great leader because he told people what he believed—"I have a dream," he said, not, "I have a plan." Many people shared his belief that change was possible, and they decided to join him.

3 If you talk about what you believe, says Sinek, you will **attract** those who share the same beliefs. Most of us are followers, but that does not mean we are unthinking or easily led. Sinek suggests that we don't follow leaders because we have to, but because we want to. To illustrate this, he points out that thousands of people didn't turn up for King himself, but for what he—and they—believed in. "It's what they believed about America," says Sinek, "that got them to travel in a bus for eight hours to stand in the sun in Washington in the middle of August."

4 Organizations, says Sinek, can also inspire followers by focusing on beliefs. The most successful businesses do more than just describe the **features** and benefits of their products. Apple, for instance, communicates its belief in thinking differently and challenging the way things are normally done. This helps to explain, says Sinek, why people stood in line for six hours when the first iPhone came out. They did this not only because of the technology, but because they wanted to be part of a company they believed in. **In other words**, says Sinek, "people don't buy *what* you do, they buy *why* you do it."

NOT ALL LEADERS INSPIRE

5 So we make our choices based on why companies and individuals do what they do. Unless we feel a real connection to the leaders in our lives—and share in their beliefs—we won't follow them. In the end, everyone wants to be part of something they believe in. "Because there are leaders and then there are those who lead," says Sinek. "Leaders hold a position of power or authority, but those who lead inspire us [. . .] We follow those who lead, not for them but for ourselves."

---

unthinking: *adj.* acting or speaking without thinking first

South African leader of the African National Congress movement, Nelson Mandela, salutes a crowd in Amsterdam in 1990.

Customers wait in line outside an Apple store for the new iPhone.

Developing Reading Skills

GETTING THE MAIN IDEAS

Use the information from the passage on pages 10–12 to answer each question.

1. What is the passage mainly about? Complete the sentence with your own idea.

    Successful leaders tell people _____

    _____

2. According to the passage, what is important to followers? Write a sentence with your ideas.

    _____

    _____

    _____

    _____

IDENTIFYING SUPPORTING IDEAS

Writers usually support their main ideas with extra details, called *supporting ideas*. The supporting ideas make their main ideas clearer, or more persuasive. The following phrases often introduce a supporting idea: "for example," "for instance," "to illustrate."

A. **Scan the passage and underline any words that signal a supporting idea.**

B. **Read the main ideas (1–3) below from the passage. Match them with their supporting ideas (a–c).**

    _____ 1. Great leaders focus on what they believe in. [Paragraph 2]

    _____ 2. People follow leaders who share the same beliefs as them. [Paragraph 3]

    _____ 3. Successful businesses focus on beliefs. [Paragraph 4]

    a. Apple, for instance, communicates its belief in thinking differently.

    b. For example, Martin Luther King Jr. told people "I have a dream," not "I have a plan."

    c. To illustrate this, he points out that thousands of people didn't turn up for King himself, but for what he—and they—believed about America.

C. **Read the ideas below from the passage. Find and underline the complete sentence in the passage. Then write down if they are main ideas (MI) or supporting ideas (SI).**

_____ **1.** . . . stood in line for six hours . . .

_____ **2.** . . . attract those that share the same beliefs . . .

_____ **3.** . . . answer questions like "What's my purpose?" . . .

_____ **4.** . . . thousands of people didn't turn up for King himself . . .

_____ **5.** . . . No emails were sent out . . .

UNDERSTANDING REFERENCES

Find the following statements in the reading and write down who is being referred to by the underlined word.

1. "They answer questions like 'What's my purpose?'"

_____

2. "'It's what they believed about America,' says Sinek."

_____

3. "They did this not only because of the technology . . ."

_____

4. " . . . not for them but for ourselves."

_____

BUILDING VOCABULARY

A. **Circle the correct word or phrase to complete each sentence.**

1. Hundreds of people **stood out / showed up** at the store at midnight to buy the new iPhone.

2. Good leaders tell people why they are doing something; **in other words / stood out**, they explain what they believe.

3. Sinek says we **feature / focus** more on a leader's beliefs instead of his or her plans.

4. A business tries to **attract / purpose** new customers by offering them better products or services.

B. **Match the word or phrase (1–4) to the best definition (a–d).**

_____ **1.** leadership

_____ **2.** features

_____ **3.** purpose

_____ **4.** stand out

a. the important parts, qualities, or abilities that something has

b. to appear more impressive than others

c. the ability or power to lead people or an organization

d. a goal or reason

GETTING MEANING FROM CONTEXT

Read the question. Write down your answer, and then discuss your ideas with a partner.

In the passage, the writer says, "Most of us are followers, but that does not mean we are unthinking or easily led." What does "easily led" mean?

_____

_____

CRITICAL THINKING

1. Reflecting. Which leaders that you know about have the characteristics described by Sinek?

_____

_____

2. Applying. The passage illustrates how good leadership can benefit businesses. What other areas of life does this idea also apply to? Explain your answer.

_____

_____

EXPLORE MORE

Watch Simon Sinek's TED Talk "How great leaders inspire action" at TED.com. What is "The Golden Circle" model of leadership? Share your opinions of Sinek's talk with your class.

TEDTALKS

HOW TO START A MOVEMENT

DEREK SIVERS Entrepreneur, TED speaker

🔊 In 1998, Derek Sivers, a professional musician, started selling his music over the Internet. At the time, no one else was selling music this way.

Sivers taught himself programming and created a website to sell his CDs online. Soon, his musician friends saw what a good idea this was and asked him to sell their CDs, too. Sivers then set up CD Baby, an online music store. Within ten years, CD Baby was the biggest online seller of independent music.

Next, Sivers did something that surprised everyone. He sold CD Baby for $22 million, which he donated to a charity for music education. Sivers has written about and presented the lessons he learned from starting, managing, and selling a business.

In this lesson, you are going to watch Sivers's TED Talk. Use the information above to answer the questions.

1. What was CD Baby?

   _____

2. What has Sivers written and presented about?

   _____

3. Look at the photo on page 17. Can you guess what the people in the video are doing? What do you think the connection is between the video and leadership?

   _____

   _____

Sivers's **idea worth spreading** is that while leaders receive the credit for a movement, the followers are the essential driving force.

IT TAKES GUTS

PREVIEWING

A. In his talk, Sivers describes how he thinks a movement starts. Put the steps (a–f) below in the order you think a movement starts.

_____ **a.** Lots of people join in.

_____ **b.** One person joins the leader.

_____ **c.** Now it's a movement.

_____ **d.** Another few people join.

_____ **e.** A leader begins a new idea alone.

_____ **f.** A second person joins in.

B. Read the excerpt from Sivers's talk. Use the context to match each bold word or phrase (1–5) with a synonym (a–e). Then watch (▶) this segment of Sivers's talk, and check your answers to Exercises A and B.

_____ **a.** completely changes

_____ **b.** accepts

_____ **c.** very important

_____ **d.** requires courage

_____ **e.** try to be like; copy

❝ First, of course you know, a leader **(1) needs the guts** to stand out and be ridiculed. But what he's doing is so easy to follow. So here's his first follower with a **(2) crucial** role; he's going to show everyone else how to follow.

Now, notice that the leader **(3) embraces** him as an equal. So, now it's not about the leader anymore; it's about them, plural. Now, there he is calling to his friends. Now, if you notice that the first follower is actually an underestimated form of leadership in itself. It takes guts to stand out like that. The first follower is what **(4) transforms** a lone nut into a leader.

And here comes a second follower. Now it's not a lone nut, it's not two nuts—three is a crowd, and a crowd is news. So a movement must be public. It's important to show not just the leader, but the followers, because you find that new followers **(5) emulate** the followers, not the leader. ❯❯

---

to be ridiculed: *v.* to be laughed at by others in a way that isn't kind

underestimate: *v.* to judge something as being less big or important than it really is

nut: *n. (informal),* a person who is strange or crazy

GETTING THE MAIN IDEA

A. **Read the statements and decide whether they are T (True) or F (False).**

_____ **1.** A leader has to be brave and not worry about being laughed at.

_____ **2.** A movement is formed as soon as one person joins a leader.

_____ **3.** Those who join a movement later do not need as much courage.

B. **According to Sivers, what might be the result of not joining in the movement? Note down your answer and discuss with a partner.**

CRITICAL THINKING

Reflecting. Would you have gotten up to dance? Would you have been the leader or a follower? Discuss your answers with a partner.

PART 2

WHO GETS THE CREDIT?

PREVIEWING

Read the excerpt from Sivers's talk. Underline who Sivers thinks gets the most credit for starting a new movement.

> The biggest lesson, if you noticed—Did you catch it?—is that leadership is over-glorified. That, yes, it was the shirtless guy who was first, and he'll get all the credit, but it was really the first follower that transformed the lone nut into a leader.

get the credit: _idiom_ to receive praise for something you have done or said

RECOGNIZING MAIN IDEAS

A. **Watch (▶) the rest of Sivers's talk. Choose which statement best summarizes Sivers's conclusion.**

_____ **a.** Nobody really understands how movements actually start.

_____ **b.** In most cases, followers don't contribute much to starting a movement.

_____ **c.** Leaders are not more important than their followers.

B. **Complete the scale to show the level of risk you think was taken by the people in the YouTube video. Then compare your answers with a partner's.**

1. leader
2. first follower
3. next followers

4. the rest of the crowd
5. non-followers

low risk ←——————————————————————————→ high risk

GETTING MEANING FROM CONTEXT

Read the excerpt below from Sivers's talk. Then write down your answer to the question.

❝ So, notice that, as more people join in, it's less risky. So those that were sitting on the fence before, now have no reason not to. . . . Now we've got momentum. This is the tipping point. Now we've got a movement. ❞

What do "sitting on the fence" and "the tipping point" mean? How else could you express these ideas?

_____

_____

IDENTIFYING TONE AND ATTITUDE

Work with a partner. What do you think Sivers's attitude is toward his topic? How would you describe his tone during the talk? Explain your answer.

_____ 1. serious   _____ 2. neutral   _____ 3. humorous

CRITICAL THINKING

Synthesizing. How do Sivers's ideas about leadership compare with Sinek's in Lesson A? What are the lessons for leaders? What are the lessons for you? Note down your answers and then discuss with a partner.

_____

_____

EXPLORE MORE

Watch another TED Talk by Derek Sivers called "Keep your goals to yourself" at TED.com. What does he mean by "a social reality"? Do you agree with him? Share your opinions with your class.

Project

The Live Aid concert in 1985, a movement started by two pop singers, benefited people suffering from famine in Africa.

A. **Work with a partner. You are going to describe how movements are created.**

1. With your partner, choose from the following movements:

   - The evolution of rap music
   - The rise of street art
   - Slow food
   - A movement where you live

2. Research the movement. Try to find answers to the following questions:

   - Did many people follow this movement at the very beginning?
   - What was the *tipping point*? In other words, when did the movement start to be popular?
   - Is this movement still popular today? Why, or why not?
   - Has it changed over time? If so, how?

3. Create a two-minute presentation. Include a timeline to show how this movement was created.

B. **Work with two other pairs. Give your presentations. As you listen to the other presentations, take notes on the following questions:**

   - Were these movements created in similar or different ways?
   - Who do you think was more important in these movements: the leaders or the followers? Why?
   - What beliefs did the leaders of the movements communicate?

EXPLORE MORE

Watch more TED Talks on leadership. Search for the "How Leaders Inspire" playlist at TED.com. What kinds of people become leaders? Which ones failed? Share what you learn with your class.

Suspended twelve stories above the forest floor, a photographer captures a view of the rain forest canopy in the Amazon, Brazil.

FRAGILE
FORESTS

GOALS

IN THIS UNIT, YOU WILL:

- Read about the threat to the canopy layer of rain forests.
- Learn how a forest ecologist is trying to help.
- Explore other conservation projects.

THINK AND DISCUSS

1. What are some ways that rain forests benefit the world?

2. Rain forests are being destroyed by human activity. Do you know any reasons why?

PRE-READING

A. Look at the diagram on page 26, and answer the questions below. Then discuss your answers with a partner.

1. How do you think the top and bottom layers of the rain forest are different?

   _____

   _____

2. Many of the rain forest's plants and animals live in the canopy. Why do you think that is?

   _____

   _____

B. Look at the photo on this page. What do you think she is doing and why? Discuss with a partner.

C. The words below come from the reading passage. Look up any words you don't know in a dictionary. What do you think you are going to read about? Discuss with a partner.

mosses	scientist
destruction	hot-air balloons
big industry	regenerate
canopy	rappers

Scientist Nalini Nadkarni uses ropes and a harness to climb to the top layers of the rain forest canopy.

1 In the rain forests of Costa Rica, scientist Nalini Nadkarni climbs a giant strangler fig tree to reach the canopy **layer**. The canopy, she says, is "like the atmosphere of an open field." Home to thousands of unique plant species, rain forests are important to the health of our planet. But the canopy layer is in trouble.

THE MYSTERIOUS CANOPY

2 As a forest ecologist, Nadkarni uses mountain-climbing techniques, construction cranes, and hot-air balloons to research life in the **mysterious** canopy. High up in the canopy layer, she studies a special group of

TROUBLE FOR THE AIR PLANTS

Unusual plants grow at the top of the rain forest. But how can they survive the destruction of their home?

plants called *epiphytes*. Worldwide, there are over 28,000 species of epiphytes, and mosses are the most common type. Epiphytes are sometimes called "air plants" because most do not have roots in the ground. Also, many of them live more than 100 feet (over 30 meters) above the forest floor. So how do these unusual plants **survive**?

3 Epiphyte roots **attach** to the branches of other plants, particularly trees. However, epiphytes don't take nutrients from their host tree. Instead, they absorb water and nutrients from the atmosphere. Nadkarni says that epiphytes have "a tremendous **capacity** for holding on to nutrients and water." Some host trees take some of these nutrients, too, through tiny roots that grow out of their branches. Because they grow so high in the canopy, epiphytes are also able to get energy from the sun.

CLINGING TO LIFE

4 These canopy communities of epiphytes are fragile; epiphytes need a specific balance of light, nutrients, and water to survive. In recent years, humans have destroyed many rain forests to make room for agriculture and other activities. This has changed the balance of light, nutrients, and water in the environment. Nadkarni says that epiphytes are an essential part of the rain forest, and not just "insignificant bits of green." Epiphytes play a vital part in keeping the climate stable. They keep the rain forests cooler and wetter by storing and then releasing huge amounts of water.

5 In the temperate rain forests of the Pacific Northwest, epiphytes are facing problems of a different kind. There, mosses are stripped from the trees and sold to florists and garden centers. It's a big industry that supplies jobs

and income for the region. Unfortunately, these mosses take a long time—over 20 years—to regenerate. Once they are **damaged**, mosses cannot easily grow back. Farming epiphytes is not **sustainable**, so Nadkarni wondered, "What can I, as an ecologist, do about that?"

RECONNECTING PEOPLE

6 Nadkarni realized that it wasn't enough to tell other scientists about the problems in the rain forests. She needed to reach out to the general public. Over the past few years, she has developed **innovative** projects to "reconnect people with trees." She has worked with rappers, writers, and artists to capture the attention of young people in particular. Through these projects, Nadkarni is spreading the word about the importance of epiphytes and the world's forest canopies.

---

fragile: *adj.* easily damaged or broken

nutrients: *n.* ingredients that plants and animals need in order to live

strip: *v.* to take off or remove

Layers of a Rain Forest

EMERGENT LAYER
High temperatures and wind limit the amount of plant and animal life here.

150–200ft

CANOPY
Home to around half of all animal and plant life in the rain forest, including epiphytes.

90–150ft

UNDERSTORY
Many insects and small animals thrive here. Limited sunshine means tree leaves are large.

3–90ft

FOREST FLOOR
Very few plants live here because it's so dark.

0–3ft

Note: The four general layers of the rain forest can vary, depending on changes in light, temperature, and wind.

Looking up to the mossy rain forest canopy, Papua, Indonesia

Developing Reading Skills

GETTING THE MAIN IDEAS

What are some of the main problems described in the passage on pages 24–26? Check (✔) all that apply.

_____ **1.** The canopy layer is too difficult to reach.

_____ **2.** Human activity is harming epiphytes.

_____ **3.** Scientists are not studying the canopy.

_____ **4.** Epiphytes are fragile and take a long time to grow.

UNDERSTANDING KEY DETAILS

What does the passage tell us about epiphytes? Complete the sentences using the words below.

canopy	forests	host	mosses
nutrients	roots	slowly	water

1. Epiphytes grow in many _____ around the world.

2. The most common epiphytes are _____.

3. Moss epiphytes often grow in the rain forest _____.

4. Their _____ attach to a _____ plant.

5. Moss epiphytes take _____ and _____ from the atmosphere.

6. They grow very _____.

A moss epiphyte

SCANNING FOR INFORMATION

When you need to find specific information in a text, you can quickly scan for clues. For example, if you need to find the name of a person or place, scan for proper nouns within sentences. If you need to find numerical information, look for numbers together with percentages or units of time, weight, or other units of measurement.

Find the information in the passage on pages 24–26 to answer the questions.

1. How many species of epiphytes are there in the world?

    _____

2. What is the height of most epiphytes above the forest floor?

    _____

3. How long does it take for stripped epiphytes to grow back?

    _____

BUILDING VOCABULARY

A. **Choose the best option or options to answer each question.**

    1. Which three of these are you most likely to describe as **innovative**?

        a. a technique   **c.** an idea

        b. a rain forest   **d.** a design

    2. Which three of these would you be likely to **attach** to a wall?

        a. a painting   **c.** a book

        b. a mirror   **d.** a shelf

    3. Which three of these sources of energy are not **sustainable**?

        a. solar power   **c.** coal

        b. oil   **d.** gas

    4. Which of these has the most **capacity**?

        a. a cup   **c.** a bathtub

        b. a jug   **d.** a swimming pool

B. **Complete the paragraph about the giant strangler fig. Use the correct form of the words below.**

damage   layers   mysterious   survive

A giant strangler fig is a _____ type of epiphyte that grows in tropical rain forests. The plant's life begins, like other epiphytes, in the top few _____ of a tree. Its roots grow slowly around the host tree. At the beginning, the host tree and strangler fig do well together. But eventually the roots of the strangler fig _____ the tree's branches. The host tree sometimes does not _____. When the host tree dies, the strangler fig can still stand up by itself.

The giant strangler fig is a type of epiphyte.

UNDERSTANDING MEANING FROM CONTEXT

Choose the definition that is closer in meaning to the phrase in bold.

1. "She has worked with rappers, writers, and artists to **capture the attention** of young people in particular."

   a. demand their support

   b. inspire them to notice

2. "Through these and other projects, Nalini Nadkarni is **spreading the word** about the importance of epiphytes and the world's forest canopies."

   a. writing lots of letters

   b. letting people know

CRITICAL THINKING

1. Reasoning. What are the best ways to capture people's attention about threats to the world's rain forests? How would you spread the word about possible solutions? Discuss with a partner.

2. Interpreting. Nadkarni says she wants to "reconnect people with trees." What does she mean, and why do you think this is important to her? Discuss with a partner.

EXPLORE MORE

Find out more about the animals and other plants that live in the canopy layer. Go to nationalgeographic.com and search for rain forests. Share what you learn with your class.

TEDTALKS

CONSERVING THE CANOPY

NALINI NADKARNI Forest ecologist, TED speaker

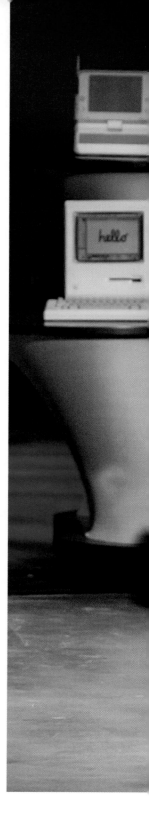

 As a child, Nalini Nadkarni grew up climbing trees for fun. Today, as a forest ecologist, she communicates her passion for trees to non-scientists—with the help of poets, musicians, and artists.

One such non-scientist is the dance director Jodi Lomask. After spending time in the Costa Rican rain forest with Nadkarni, Lomask felt inspired. With her dance troupe, Capacitor, she created an amazing dance called Biome.

After this successful collaboration, Nadkarni set up the Sound Science project. Together with rap artist C.A.U.T.I.O.N., she brought middle-school students from the inner city to experience the rain forest canopy for themselves. Then they composed their own rap songs, which they recorded in a studio afterwards.

Nadkarni wants everyone to know how beautiful and how necessary the forest canopy is. Through these projects, she has been able to get others to see this, too. "The results have been fantastic," she says.

In this lesson, you are going to watch segments of Nadkarni's talk. Use the information above to answer the questions.

1. How did Nadkarni's interest in trees begin?

_____

Nadkarni's **idea worth spreading** is that canopies are important to our world, and should be protected, because they promote biodiversity and keep our global climate stable.

2. Why did Jodi Lomask create a dance called Biome?

_____

3. Who participated in the Sound Science project with C.A.U.T.I.O.N.?

_____

JOURNEY TO THE CANOPY

PREVIEWING

In the first part of Nadkarni's talk, she shows what it's like to climb up to the rain forest canopy. What do you think she sees as she climbs up? Write down some ideas.

_____

RECOGNIZING PURPOSE

A. Watch (▶) the first segment of Nadkarni's talk and check your ideas from the Previewing activity.

B. Why do you think she shows the audience a clip of herself climbing up to the canopy? Choose the best answer.

   a. To highlight the beauty of the canopy

   b. To highlight the size of the canopy

   c. To highlight the danger of the canopy

C. Read the excerpt below from Nadkarni's talk. Then choose the two best answers to the question.

   ❝ I'd like to take you all on a journey up to the forest canopy, and share with you what canopy researchers are asking and also how they're communicating with other people outside of science. ❞

   What do you think the canopy researchers like Nadkarni are asking questions about?

   a. How to encourage more people to visit the canopy

   b. How the problems in the canopy layer can be solved

   c. How epiphytes can be removed from the canopy layer

CRITICAL THINKING

Reasoning. What challenges do you think the filmmakers faced while filming Nadkarni's journey to the canopy? How do you think they overcame these challenges? Discuss with a partner.

SAVING THE MOSSES

PREVIEWING

A. In Lesson A, you learned about the problems facing moss epiphytes in the Pacific Northwest. What solution do you think Nadkarni might have for this particular problem? Discuss with a partner.

B. Scan this excerpt from Nadkarni's talk. What words do you think are missing? Write one word in each space and share with a partner.

> ❝ My thought was that I could learn how to (1) _____ mosses, and that way we wouldn't have to take them out of the wild. And I thought, if I had some partners that could (2) _____ me with this, that would be great. And so, I thought perhaps incarcerated men and women—who don't have access to (3) _____, who often have a lot of (4) _____, they often have space, and you don't need any sharp tools to work with mosses—would be great partners. ❞

incarcerated: *adj.* kept in prison

UNDERSTANDING THE MAIN IDEAS

A. Watch (▶) this segment of the talk and check your answers to the Previewing activities above. Who helped Nadkarni grow mosses?

_____

B. Read the excerpt below. Underline the different projects Nadkarni started at the prison.

> ❝ We've been successful as partners in figuring out which species grow the fastest, and I've just been overwhelmed with how successful this has been. Because the prison wardens were very enthusiastic about this as well, I started a science and sustainability seminar in the prisons. I brought my scientific colleagues . . . into the prison. We gave talks once a month, and that actually ended up implementing some amazing sustainability projects at the prisons—organic gardens, worm culture, recycling, water catchment, and beekeeping. ❞

overwhelmed: *adj.* very strongly affected (emotionally) by something

enthusiastic: *adj.* feeling or showing a lot of excitement and interest in something

implementing: *v.* putting a plan into action

C. **What is this part of Nadkarni's talk mostly about? Choose the best statement.**

1. Prisoners learned how to grow epiphytes.

2. Nadkarni gave a presentation about trees to prisoners.

3. Nadkarni created a sustainability program at a prison.

RECOGNIZING SUPPORTING EVIDENCE

Writers and speakers often support their ideas with supporting evidence, such as examples, statistics, and comparisons.

A. **Read the excerpts from Nadkarni's talk below. Then write whether each piece of supporting evidence is an example, a statistic, or a comparison.**

1. "It's a 265-million-dollar industry, and it's increasing rapidly." _____

2. "They learned how to distinguish different species of mosses, which . . . is a lot more

   than my undergraduate students at the Evergreen College can do." _____

3. "[They implemented] amazing sustainability projects at the prisons—organic gardens,

   worm culture, recycling, water catchment, and beekeeping." _____

B. **Underline the specific parts of the sentences in Exercise A that helped you to decide on your answers.**

CRITICAL THINKING

1. Inferring. Why do you think the wardens liked the project? Discuss with a partner.

2. Synthesis. In Unit 1, Derek Sivers talks about starting a movement. Do you think Nalini Nadkarni is starting a movement, too? If so, who are her followers? Write down your ideas and then discuss them with a partner.

_____

_____

EXPLORE MORE

Watch Nadkarni's full TED Talk at TED.com. Share what you learn about her other conservation projects with your classmates.

Project

Nadkarni gives a presentation about trees to inmates in Cedar Creek Corrections in Littlerock, Washington, U.S.A.

A.   Work with a partner. You are going to research a sustainability project.

1. With your partner, decide whether you want your project to be about:
    - a global conservation project
    - a local initiative in your area or school

2. Create a short report about your chosen sustainability project. Make sure you remember to do the following:
    - Give your report a title.
    - Begin with a strong statement of the issue—one sentence that will capture people's attention.
    - Briefly describe the project in two short paragraphs.
    - Provide supporting evidence (examples, graphics, etc.) to help people understand the issue.
    - Inspire people by describing the possible benefits of the project.
    - End the report with a short summary sentence.

B.   Work with two other pairs. Share your reports. Which sustainability project are you most likely to join? Why?

EXPLORE MORE

Find out more about Nalini Nadkarni's prison project. Watch her other TED Talk called "Life science in prison" at TED.com. What else did you learn about the project? Share your ideas with a partner.

A group of women using solar-powered lanterns pick flowers at night in India.

BRIGHT IDEAS

GOALS

IN THIS UNIT, YOU WILL:

- Read about simple inventions that make people's lives better.
- Learn about an invention that is saving babies' lives.
- Explore other simple and creative solutions that improve or save lives.

THINK AND DISCUSS

1. What do you think is the most useful invention ever created? What problem did it solve?

2. What are some big problems that we don't have solutions for yet? Rank them in order of importance.

Lesson A

PRE-READING

Look at the photos and infographic and read the captions on pages 38-41. Then answer the questions below before discussing with a partner.

Liquid Lenses

1. What do you think their purpose is?

   _____

2. How do you think they work?

   _____

Fuel Briquettes

1. What do you think their purpose is?

   _____

2. Where do you think they are used?

   _____

3. Who do you think uses them?

   _____

Disaster Shelters

1. What do you think their purpose is?

   _____

2. Where do you think they could be used?

   _____

3. What problems do you think they solve?

   _____

BIG PROBLEMS, SIMPLE SOLUTIONS

Ingenious innovations are improving health and well-being in communities around the world. Speakers at recent TED events have shared simple and inexpensive solutions that can solve everyday problems.

LIQUID LENSES

1 Many people need eyeglasses, but there often aren't enough eye doctors in the developing world. For example, there's only one optometrist for every 8 million people in some parts of Africa. Physicist Joshua Silver has a solution: **Adjust** your own eyeglasses.

2 Silver invented eyeglasses that have lenses filled with a liquid. You turn a dial on the sides of the glasses to add or subtract the liquid. Adjusting the amount of liquid changes the strength of the lenses, making it easier for people to see better. The glasses cost $19 today, but Silver hopes to get this down to $1 by 2020.

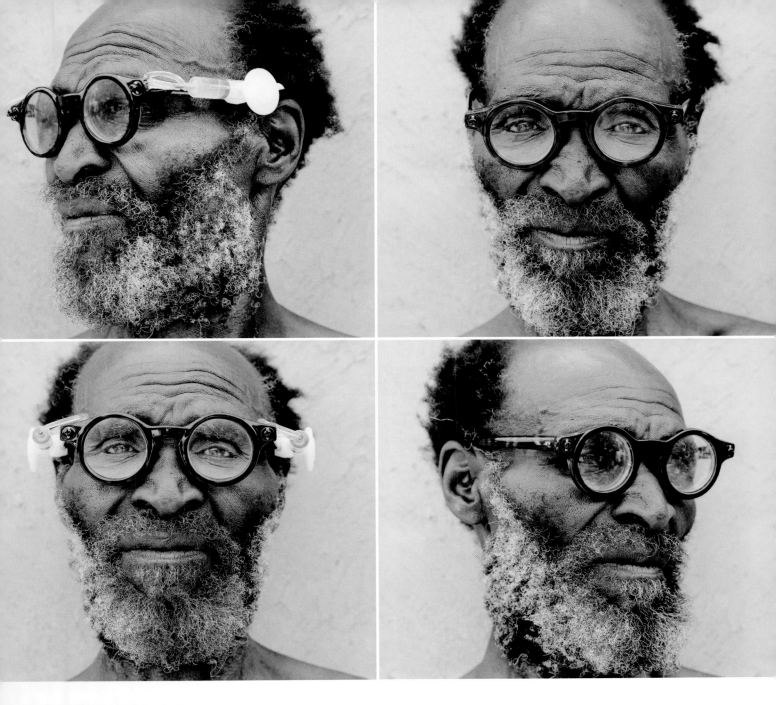

FUEL BRIQUETTES

3 In the developing world, smoke from indoor cooking kills more than 2 million children each year. In fact, it's the number one cause of death of children under five. Amy Smith, founder of D-Lab at the Massachusetts Institute of Technology (MIT), discovered a way to make a safe cooking fuel. The material she uses is also free and **plentiful**: farm waste.

4 Smith invented a low-cost **device** that compresses farm waste into fuel briquettes. These briquettes produce smoke that is less dangerous than the smoke from other fuel, such as wood. They also burn hotter and last longer. Farmers can make these briquettes from readily **available** waste, such as hay in India and corncobs in Ghana. This innovation has an economic benefit, too. Farmers can buy the press for $2 and sell briquettes they don't use. Smith **estimates** that this can increase a farmer's income by $500 a month.

---

compresses: *v.* presses together

portable: *adj.* movable, capable of being carried or moved around

DISASTER SHELTERS

5 Over 31 million people worldwide lose their homes every year due to natural disasters such as hurricanes and earthquakes. After these disasters, many people live in terrible conditions—in tents or in large arenas with no privacy. Graphic designer Michael McDaniel invented inexpensive, **temporary** housing for people in these situations.

6 Called the Reaction Exo, these shelters are small, one-room houses that comfortably hold up to four people. They're made from a plastic that is strong, recyclable, and super light. In fact, they're so light that you can lift them by hand. The shelters are very **portable**—you can stack them like paper cups to transport them easily. They snap together, so you can make one large shelter with several rooms. McDaniel hopes that his invention will provide an **affordable** solution to help people rebuild their lives after a natural disaster.

SHIPPING: COMPARISON

20 Reaction Exos
80 People housed

vs.

2 Travel Trailers
8 People housed

vs.

1 Shipping Container
6 People housed

SETUP: 2 MINUTES OR LESS

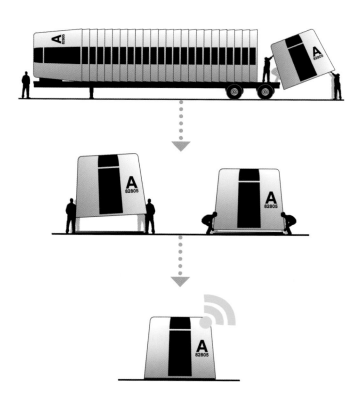

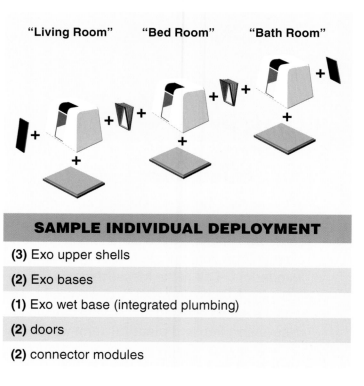

"Living Room"   "Bed Room"   "Bath Room"

SAMPLE INDIVIDUAL DEPLOYMENT

(3) Exo upper shells

(2) Exo bases

(1) Exo wet base (integrated plumbing)

(2) doors

(2) connector modules

Hellen Esaete dries agricultural waste briquettes at the Teso Women Development Initiatives in Soroti District, Uganda. Hellen uses the proceeds from selling the briquettes to pay her school fees.

Developing Reading Skills

GETTING THE MAIN IDEAS

A. **What do you think the passage is mainly about? Choose the best statement.**

a. Sometimes, common problems can be solved inexpensively.

b. Advanced technology can help solve some common problems.

c. Big corporations have solved some common problems.

B. **Check (✓) three of the statements below that best describe the benefits of all of the inventions in the passage.**

_____ **a.** They are inexpensive.

_____ **b.** They improve or save lives.

_____ **c.** They use local materials.

_____ **d.** They are easy to use.

UNDERSTANDING KEY DETAILS

Complete the chart with details about the three inventions described in the passage on pages 38–40.

1. Liquid lenses

2. Farm waste

3. Lightweight and easy to transport

4. Smoke from indoor cooking

5. Amy Smith

6. Liquid

7. Michael McDaniel

8. Plastic

9. Easy to adjust lenses

10. Fuel briquettes

11. Poor shelters for disaster victims

12. Not enough optometrists

Problem	Solution	Inventor	Main Material	Main Benefit
		Joshua Silver		
				Cleaner burning
	Disaster shelters			

UNDERSTANDING VISUALS

Look at the infographic on page 40 and answer the questions.

1. What is the main purpose of the infographic? Check (✓) the two best answers.

   _____ **a.** To show how quickly an Exo shelter can be set up

   _____ **b.** To show how much an Exo shelter costs to build

   _____ **c.** To show how easy it is to transport several Exo shelters

2. How many people can the following types of shelter hold?

   a. 20 Exos: _____

   b. Two travel trailers: _____

   c. One shipping container: _____

3. How long does it take to set up an Exo?

   _____

MAKING INFERENCES

Writers sometimes suggest ideas, but they don't state them directly. Readers must infer these ideas.

Check (✓) which of the following statements can be inferred from the passage.

_____ **1.** An optometrist is a type of doctor who treats eye conditions.

_____ **2.** Only the richest people in some parts of Africa can be treated by an eye doctor.

_____ **3.** Joshua Silver feels his eyeglasses will be more successful if they're cheaper.

_____ **4.** Silver likely got his idea for the eyeglasses while he was a university researcher.

_____ **5.** Amy Smith hoped to reduce the number of deaths caused by indoor cooking.

_____ **6.** Wood is a commonly used fuel in developing countries.

_____ **7.** Smith's fuel briquettes have been most successful so far in India and Ghana.

_____ **8.** The Exo disaster shelter offers more privacy than other disaster shelters.

_____ **9.** Michael McDaniel thinks the Exo disaster shelter could also be used as a permanent housing alternative.

BUILDING VOCABULARY

A. Complete the sentences with the correct form of the words below.

| adjust | affordable | estimate | plentiful |

1. The self-adjusting eyeglasses might cost only $1. This makes them very _____.

2. It's practical to use farm waste to make briquettes because it's very _____. There's a lot of it everywhere in the world.

3. People can _____ the lenses on Silver's eyeglasses by themselves.

4. Smith isn't sure how much money farmers can make by selling the fuel briquettes, but

   she _____ that it might be around $500 a month.

B. Complete each statement with the correct word.

1. If something is **temporary**, it is there for a ____ amount of time.

   a. long   **b.** short

2. If something is **available**, it's ____ to get.

   a. hard   **b.** easy

3. Another word for **device** is "____."

   a. idea   **b.** equipment

4. If something is **portable**, it is ____ to carry around.

   a. easy   **b.** hard

GETTING MEANING FROM CONTEXT

A. Find the phrase "get this down to" in paragraph 2. What do you think it means?

     a. to lower an amount   **b.** to sell something in more places   **c.** to make something shorter

B. The passage mentions that the fuel briquettes have an "economic benefit." What does this phrase mean? Discuss with a partner.

CRITICAL THINKING

Evaluating. Which of the three inventions do you think could be the most useful for your country? Why?

_____

EXPLORE MORE

Learn more about Silver's, Smith's, and McDaniel's inventions by watching their TED Talks at TED.com. Find out more places where people are using these innovations. Share your information with the class.

TEDTALKS

A WARM EMBRACE THAT SAVES LIVES

JANE CHEN Social entrepreneur, TED speaker

In 2008, Jane Chen went to India with the goal of solving a terrible problem: infant mortality. More than a quarter of infant deaths in the world occur in India, and many of these deaths occur because a baby is born premature.

Premature babies can't regulate their own body temperatures because they don't have enough fat to stay warm. Because they can't keep warm, the babies are not able to grow properly. Those babies that do survive sometimes grow up with long-term health problems such as diabetes or heart disease.

Many of these problems could be prevented if premature babies were kept warm. Chen spent time talking to mothers and health workers in India. She quickly realized that expensive, high-tech solutions—such as incubators—were not the answer. As Chen says, she wanted to help people by creating a more "human-centered design."

---

mortality: *n.* the rate of death from illness

premature: *adj.* born too early

regulate: *v.* control

incubator: *n.* a special hospital bed with a cover, used to warm babies

In this lesson, you are going to watch Chen's TED Talk. Use the information about Chen above to answer the questions.

1. What health problem did Jane Chen study in India?

   _____

2. Why do premature babies sometimes develop health issues later in life?

   _____

   _____

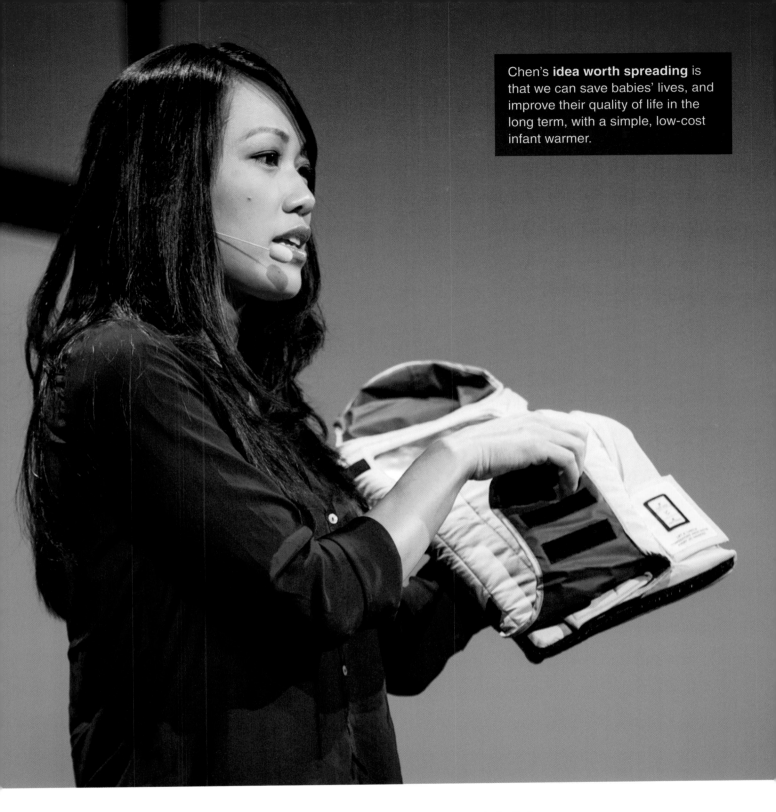

Chen's **idea worth spreading** is that we can save babies' lives, and improve their quality of life in the long term, with a simple, low-cost infant warmer.

3. Why do you think an expensive, high-tech solution is not the answer in India?

_____

_____

A BIG PROBLEM

PREVIEWING

Complete the excerpt from Chen's talk with the words below.

electricity	hot-water bottles	light bulbs	rural	unsafe

❝ . . . [T]raditional incubators require _____ and cost up to $20,000. So, you're not

going to find them in _____ areas of developing countries. As a result, parents resort

to local solutions like tying _____ around their babies' bodies, or placing them under

_____—methods that are both ineffective and _____. . . . ❞

---

resort to: *v.* do something extreme because of limited choices

IDENTIFYING SOLUTIONS

A. **Watch (▶) the first segment of Chen's TED Talk and check your answers to the Previewing activity. Then answer the question below.**

What two solutions have local people tried in the past? Why do you think these solutions don't work? Discuss with a partner.

B. **Read the excerpt below. Then choose the three best features for a local solution to the problem.**

❝ [M]y team and I realized what was needed was a local solution, something that could work without electricity, that was simple enough for a mother or a midwife to use, given that the majority of births still take place in the home. We needed something that was portable, something that could be sterilized and reused across multiple babies, and something ultra low-cost . . . ❞

---

midwife: *n.* a person whose job is to help women when they are giving birth

sterilize: *v.* to make completely free of dirt and germs

Chen realized the solution to the problem should be ____, ____, and ____.

1. powered with electricity

4. attractively designed

2. easy to move around

5. made from recycled materials

3. affordable

6. easy to clean

CRITICAL THINKING

1. Synthesizing. How are the problems Chen describes similar to the ones described in the passage in Lesson A?

_____

_____

2. Predicting. How do you think Chen solved the problem of keeping premature babies warm?

_____

_____

PART 2

A BETTER SOLUTION

UNDERSTANDING DETAILS

Read the following excerpt from Chen's talk and answer the questions (1–3). Then watch (▶) this segment of her talk to check your answers.

❝ What you see here looks nothing like an incubator. It looks like a small sleeping bag for a baby. You can open it up completely. It's waterproof. There's no seams inside so you can sterilize it very easily. But the magic is in this pouch of wax. This is a phase-change material. It's a wax-like substance with a melting point of human body temperature, 37 degrees Celsius. You can melt this simply using hot water and then when it melts it's able to maintain one constant temperature for four to six hours at a time, after which you simply reheat the pouch. So, you then place it into this little pocket back here, and it creates a warm micro-environment for the baby.

Looks simple, but we've reiterated this dozens of times by going into the field to talk to doctors, moms, and clinicians to ensure that this really meets the needs of the local communities. ❯❯

---

seams: *n.* lines where two pieces of cloth are sewed together

phase-change material: *n.* a substance that changes in some way; for example, from a solid to a liquid

1. What is the phase-change material?

   a. Something like water

   b. Something like wax

2. What happens when the phase-change material melts?

   a. It gets to the same temperature as the human body.

   b. It sterilizes the pouch.

3. Why is this phase-change material useful for Chen's invention?

   _____

VISUALIZING A PROCESS

Use the diagram and the words below to complete the sentences about how the Embrace works. One item is extra.

37 degrees	**4–6 hours**	**baby**	**phase-change material**	**pocket**

1. Melt the _____.

2. When it's _____, put the material in a _____ in the device.

3. Wrap the _____ in the device.

4. Reheat the material after _____.

heating pad or hot water

phase-change material

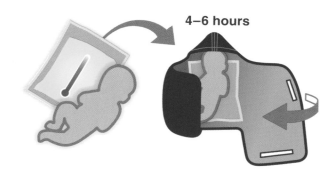

4–6 hours

CRITICAL THINKING

Interpreting. In her talk, Chen says that her invention will also reduce population growth. Why does she think this will happen?

_____

_____

EXPLORE MORE

Find out more about Chen's invention at TED.com. Share your information with the class.

Project

A student tries a LifeStraw water purifier at the Kimanza Secondary School in Matungula District, Kenya.

A. **Work with a partner. You are going to find out about other low-cost innovations that improve or save lives.**

1. Go to TED.com and watch the following TED Talks.

   - R.A. Mashelkar: "Breakthrough designs for ultra low-cost products"
   - Anil Gupta: "India's hidden hotbeds of invention"
   - Michael Pritchard: "How to make filthy water drinkable"

2. With your partner, choose one of the talks and answer these questions about it.

   - What is the problem?
   - Where does it occur?
   - What is the solution?
   - How does it work?
   - Why is it a good solution to the problem?

3. Use your information to create a two-minute presentation. You can use maps, photos, and video to explain your information.

B. **Work with two other pairs who chose a different innovation and complete the steps below.**

   - Give your presentation.
   - As you listen, take notes.
   - At the end, review your notes.
   - Discuss: Which innovation seems the most useful or important? Why?

EXPLORE MORE

Learn more about simple solutions to big problems at TED.com. What is another useful innovation you found? Share what you learn with your class.

GOALS

IN THIS UNIT, YOU WILL:

- Read about the benefits of playing games online.
- Learn about how online gamers could help save the world.

THINK AND DISCUSS

1. Do you play games online? What are some online games people play?

2. Why do you think online gaming is popular?

GAME CHANGERS

Online gamers—people who play interactive games online—test a new online game at the E3 Electronic Entertainment Expo in Los Angeles, U.S.A.

PRE-READING

A. **Read the caption at the top of page 53. What skills do you think you need to be successful in a game like this? Discuss your ideas with a partner.**

B. **Look at the infographic on page 54 and answer the questions below.**

   1. What does the infographic tell you about the number, type, and location of gamers in the world?

   _____

   _____

   2. What information surprises or interests you?

   _____

   _____

C. **Look at the title of the passage. How would you answer the question in the title? Discuss with a partner.**

D. **Now skim the whole passage quickly. Does Jane McGonigal think online gaming is good for us?**

   _____

IS GAMING GOOD FOR YOU?

1 Researchers who study online gaming have shown that it is more than just a **form** of entertainment. In fact, people may benefit from online gaming in a number of ways. For example, multiplayer online gaming can improve social skills because players have to work together toward the same goals. In one study, researchers in the Netherlands surveyed teens who played *World of Warcraft*. They found that the more frequently most teens played, the more socially successful and less lonely they felt.

2 Online gaming may also improve thinking skills. In a recent study in Berlin, adults played a video game every day for two months.

A screen shot of the multiplayer online game *World of Warcraft*. Gamers control an avatar and interact with other avatars during the game.

An "epic win"—winning a game in a way that seems impossible until it happens—is a great feeling. But can it help gamers solve real-world problems?

Afterwards, researchers scanned the players' brains. They noticed that the players had more neurons in the parts of the brain that are responsible for memory and planning.

3 Game designer Jane McGonigal has her own ideas about the benefits of gaming—not just for individual people, but for the whole world. She calls people who play online games for at least one hour a day "virtuoso" gamers. Currently, there are about 500 million virtuoso gamers in the world. McGonigal **predicts** that in ten years there will be 1.5 billion.

4 McGonigal believes that these gamers have four **characteristics**—"superpowers"—that make them better problem solvers. These characteristics are:

- Urgent optimism: Online gamers don't *wait* to defeat a dragon. Instead, gamers face any problem immediately—and believe that they can succeed.

- Community builders: Players in an online game have the same goal—to win. They expect that everyone will play fairly and follow the same rules. This helps players build trust and improve **cooperation**.

- Blissful productivity: Gamers enjoy working hard to achieve online gaming goals. They feel a real sense of **accomplishment** when they do achieve these goals—the "epic win" feeling.

- Epic meaning: Gamers like being **involved** in an important mission. The larger-than-life worlds of online gaming make players feel that they are playing a part in a **significant** story.

5 Non-gamers may think online gaming is a waste of time and money. Some have argued online games contribute to problems like childhood obesity. However, McGonigal thinks online gamers could be an important global **resource** if we can design games that help them create "epic wins" in response to real-world problems.

GAMING BY THE NUMBERS

 1.2 BILLION the number of gamers playing worldwide. Of these, 700 million are online gamers.

 22 HOURS the average time a gamer plays *World of Warcraft* each week in the U.S.A.

 $ 70 BILLION DOLLARS the amount of money gamers spent in 2013.

18 percent

of gamers in the U.S.A. are under the age of 18

42 percent

of gamers in the U.S.A. are female

45 percent

of parents in the U.S.A. play games with their children every week

ACTIVE GAMERS VS. TOTAL POPULATION

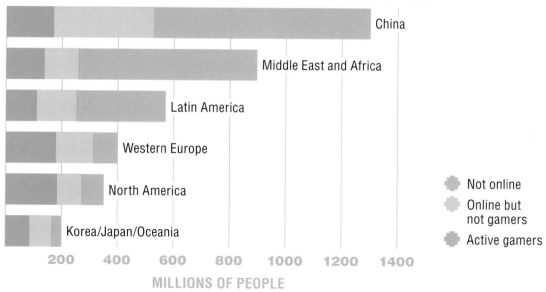

China

Middle East and Africa

Latin America

Western Europe

North America

Korea/Japan/Oceania

Not online

Online but not gamers

Active gamers

200   400   600   800   1000   1200   1400

MILLIONS OF PEOPLE

Sources: Jane McGonigal; 2013 Global Games Market Report; internap.com

10,000 hours gaming by age 21

Jane McGonigal shows a photo of a gamer about to achieve an "epic win" while playing an online game. McGonigal thinks we can design games that help create epic wins in response to real-world problems.

Developing Reading Skills

GETTING THE MAIN IDEAS

Use information from the passage on pages 52–54 to answer each question.

1. How might multiplayer online gaming improve social skills?

   _____

2. What two parts of the brain do some researchers think are improved by playing online games?

   _____

3. What particular group of gamers does McGonigal think is great at solving problems?

   _____

UNDERSTANDING KEY DETAILS

Read the statements about virtuoso gamers below, and label them *T* for True or *F* for False based on the information in the passage.

_____ 1. Virtuoso gamers can solve problems.

_____ 2. Virtuoso gamers are prepared to work hard to get an epic win.

_____ 3. Players often build trust with each other.

_____ 4. Gamers can create a community that shares the same goals.

_____ 5. Virtuoso gamers expect easy wins.

ANALYZING PROS AND CONS

To show a balanced approach, writers sometimes present both sides of an issue in their writing—the arguments for (the pros) and the arguments against (the cons).

A. Scan the passage and complete the chart with the possible pros and cons of online gaming.

Pros	Cons
1. Improves _____	4. Waste of _____
2. Improves _____	5. Waste of _____
3. Better _____	6. Contributes to childhood _____

B. Do you think the focus of the article is more about the positive side of online gaming, or the negative side? Discuss your answers with a partner.

UNDERSTANDING DATA

Look at the infographic on page 54 and answer the questions.

1. What percentage of U.S. gamers are under 18 years old?

   _____

2. On average, how many hours a week does a gamer spend playing *World of Warcraft* in the U.S.A.?

   _____

3. Which two regions of the world have the highest number of active gamers?

   _____

4. Which part of the world has the most people online?

   _____

5. Approximately how much money did people spend on gaming worldwide in 2013?

   _____

6. Did anything in the data surprise you? Discuss with a partner.

   _____

BUILDING VOCABULARY

A. **Choose the best word to complete each sentence.**

characteristics   involved   predict   significant

1. McGonigal thinks that virtuoso gamers have certain _____ that make them good at online gaming.

2. The challenges of online games, such as saving the world from aliens, can make gamers feel like they are doing something _____.

3. Some researchers find that players who are _____ in multi-player games develop stronger social skills.

4. Experts _____ that online gaming will continue to increase in popularity in the next ten years.

B. **Choose the best option(s) to answer each question.**

1. Which of these are **resources**?

   a. arguments   **b.** oil   **c.** water

2. Which of these activities requires **cooperation**?

   a. taking an exam   **b.** reading a book   **c.** playing soccer

3. Which of these events are **accomplishments**?

   a. speaking to a friend   **b.** winning a race   **c.** graduating from college

4. Which of these are usually **forms** of entertainment?

   a. a TV show   **b.** a movie director   **c.** a pop song

GETTING MEANING FROM CONTEXT

The writer mentions the "larger-than-life" worlds of online games. What do you think "larger than life" means? What makes online gaming worlds larger than life?

_____

_____

CRITICAL THINKING

1. Inferring. Why do you think more adults play video games now than they did in the past?

2. Reflecting. What other activities do you think can improve a person's social skills? What activities might improve a person's memory? What activities might improve problem-solving skills?

EXPLORE MORE

Read more about game designer Jane McGonigal at TED.com. Share what you learn with the class.

TEDTALKS

GAMING CAN MAKE A BETTER WORLD

JANE McGONIGAL Game designer, TED speaker

We spend 3 billion hours a week playing online games, but game designer Jane McGonigal thinks this isn't enough. In fact, she thinks that we should be playing online games for at least 21 billion hours a week for the next ten years.

For over ten years, McGonigal has been designing online games. She wants to convince more people to spend more time playing bigger and better games. Why? She believes that playing online games might help us solve global problems like poverty, climate change, and obesity.

In this lesson, you are going to watch segments of McGonigal's TED Talk. Read the information about McGonigal above and answer the questions.

1. How often does McGonigal think we should be playing online games?

   _____

   _____

2. What kinds of problems does McGonigal think online games can help solve?

   _____

   _____

McGonigal's **idea worth spreading** is that the skills we learn playing games can also be used to solve real-world problems.

SOLVING REAL-WORLD PROBLEMS

PREVIEWING

Read this excerpt from McGonigal's talk. What problem does she think a lot of gamers have? Note down your answers. Then discuss with a partner.

> And this is a problem that a lot of gamers have. We feel that we are not as good in reality as we are in games. And I don't mean just good as in successful, although that's part of it. We do achieve more in game worlds. But I also mean good as in motivated to do something that matters, inspired to collaborate and to cooperate.

_____

_____

GETTING THE MAIN IDEAS

A. **Watch (▶) the first segment of McGonigal's talk. Why does McGonigal think we don't often have an "epic win" face in real life?**

_____

_____

B. **Check (✓) the feelings that McGonigal thinks do not exist in game worlds.**

angry	overwhelmed	anxious	depressed
frustrated	tired	cynical	bored

C. **Read the excerpt from McGonigal's talk and complete the sentence below.**

> And the only problem is that [gamers] believe that they are capable of changing virtual worlds and not the real world. That's the problem that I'm trying to solve.

McGonigal wants to help gamers change _____.

CRITICAL THINKING

Inferring. What do you think McGonigal means when she says, "We do not want to try to predict the future. What we want to do is make the future"?

_____

_____

_____

EPIC WINS IN THE REAL WORLD

SUMMARIZING

Watch (▶) the second segment of McGonigal's talk. Complete the concept map with details about two of the three games that McGonigal describes.

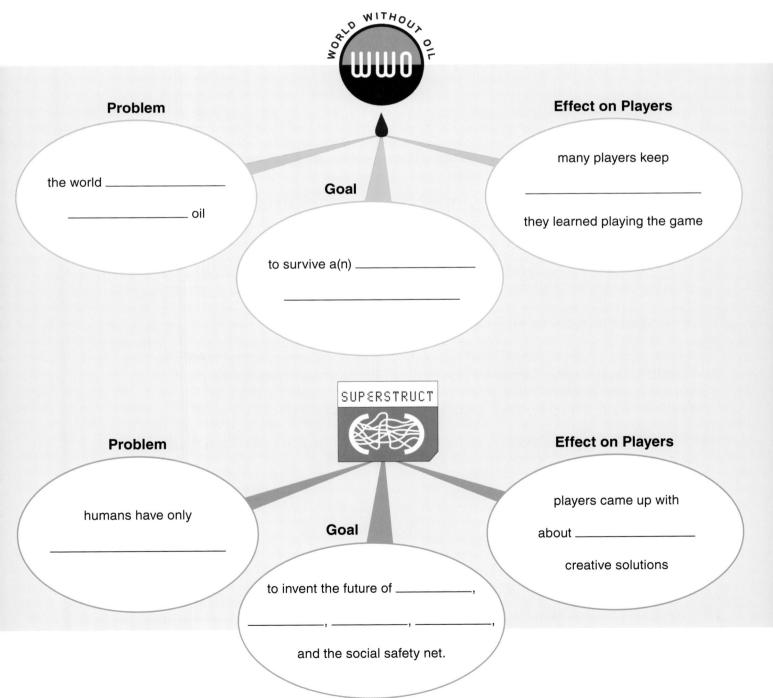

Problem

the world _____

_____ oil

Goal

to survive a(n) _____

_____

Effect on Players

many players keep

_____

they learned playing the game

WORLD WITHOUT OIL
WWO

SUPERSTRUCT

Problem

humans have only

_____

Goal

to invent the future of _____,

_____, _____, _____,

and the social safety net.

Effect on Players

players came up with

about _____

creative solutions

RECOGNIZING TONE AND MESSAGE

Read the excerpt from McGonigal's talk. Which statement below best matches McGonigal's message?

❝ I want to ask a question. What do you think happens next? We've got all these amazing gamers, we've got these games that are kind of pilots of what we might do, but none of them have saved the real world yet. Well, I hope that you will agree with me that gamers are a human resource that we can use to do real-world work, that games are a powerful platform for change. We have all these amazing superpowers: blissful productivity, the ability to weave a tight social fabric, this feeling of urgent optimism, and the desire for epic meaning. ❞

---

weave a social fabric: *idiom* create a community

_____ **1.** Games and online gamers provide a resource that could help us create the kind of world we want to live in.

_____ **2.** Gamers like to work hard, are optimistic and cooperative, and share the feeling that they are doing something important.

_____ **3.** Gamers have already shown that they can solve big, real-world problems.

CRITICAL THINKING

1. Reflecting. Would you like to play *World Without Oil* or *Superstruct*? Why or why not? Write your answer and then discuss with a partner.

_____

_____

2. Evaluating. Do you agree that gamers have "superpowers" and are a resource that we can use to solve problems? Write your answer and then discuss your reasons with a partner.

_____

_____

_____

EXPLORE MORE

Watch McGonigal's full TED Talk at TED.com. Learn more about why McGonigal thinks online game players are such good problem solvers. Share what you learn with your class.

Evoke, a social network game developed by Jane McGonigal with the World Bank, aims to empower people all over the world to come up with creative solutions to urgent social problems.

A. **Work with a partner. You and your partner have been hired by the Institute for the Future to come up with a proposal for an online game that can have a positive impact on the world.**

You need to decide:

- on a global issue. Some ideas include reducing climate change, fighting epidemics, producing enough food for everyone, improving education, disaster relief, dealing with resource shortages (water, oil, trees, etc.), and so on.
- the game's end goal; how the game works; what do gamers need to do?
- the title of the game.

B. **Work with two other pairs.**

- Give your presentation. Explain your proposal.
- As you listen, take notes.
- At the end, review your notes.
- Which proposal is the most likely to receive funding from the Institute for the Future?

EXPLORE MORE

Learn more about online gaming. Read "10 online games . . . with a social purpose" on the TED Blog at TED.com. What are some other games that help people think about big, real-world problems? How do you play them? Share your information with the class.

A boy pays close attention in a classroom
in Odisha State, India, in 1970.

LESSONS IN
LEARNING

IN THIS UNIT, YOU WILL:

- Read about making learning relevant for more students.
- Learn about the importance of perseverance in learning.
- Explore other ways to enhance

THINK AND DISCUSS

1. Why do you think some students do better in school than others?

2. How do you think students can become better learners?

PRE-READING

A. Look at the charts on page 67. Why do you think more students feel disengaged with school as they get older? Discuss with a partner.

B. Look at the information at the bottom of page 68 about The Da Vinci Studio School of Science and Technology. Then answer the questions. Discuss your answers with a partner.

1. How is the Da Vinci school different from traditional schools?

_____

_____

2. Why do you think students at this school don't have to do homework?

_____

_____

3. What do you think a "personal coach" does?

_____

_____

C. What makes some schools more appealing to students than other schools? Write some notes below and discuss with a partner.

_____

_____

_____

_____

Check your ideas as you read the article.

ENGAGING LEARNERS

1 Not all teenagers do well at school, but why is that? There are plenty of theories—poverty, I.Q., family background. But researchers are also discovering that other factors lie at the heart of student success.

High school students look at water samples on a field trip in Bayou La Branche, Louisiana, U.S.A.

2   A recent Gallup poll in the U.S.A. found that over half of all high school students do not feel **engaged** with their studies. Why? Researchers think some students do not thrive in schools that focus on teacher-centered, test-focused, and academic learning. These students often struggle to see the relationship between this kind of learning and their lives. A report from the U.K. **indicates** that nearly a third of students do not complete their education because they don't think their schooling is **relevant** to the kind of work they will do in the future.

Students' Engagement Over Time

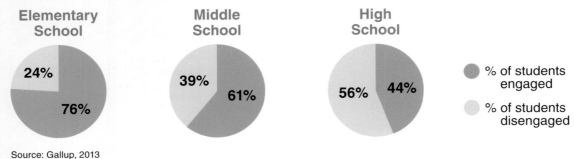

Elementary School
24%
76%

Middle School
39%
61%

High School
56%
44%

● % of students engaged

● % of students disengaged

Source: Gallup, 2013

3 How can teenage students become more engaged? Geoff Mulgan, social commentator and TED speaker, believes the solution lies in making learning more relevant. He researched how people learn in schools around the world, from Australia to Paraguay. His research suggested that a new model of schooling was needed—a model that connects what students are learning to their own plans for their future. "What kind of school would have teenagers fighting to get in, not fighting to stay out?" wondered Mulgan.

LEARNING BY DOING

4 Mulgan helped create the Studio School, a system of publicly funded schools for 14- to 19-year olds in the U.K. Unlike traditional education, Studio Schools **combine** academic learning with practical training for future jobs. About 80 percent of the curriculum is done not through sitting in classrooms but through real-life, practical projects, including working at local businesses. Mulgan points out that many teenagers "learn best in teams, and they learn best by doing things for real."

5 This different **approach** is also enhanced by more personalized instruction and support. Studio Schools are smaller than traditional schools—typically around 300 learners—to ensure that every student feels valued and supported. Each student has a "personal **coach**" who helps him or her develop a plan to meet their learning goals. By having more tangible goals, students become more **determined** to do well at school. Reports have shown **promising** results. Many traditional-school students who were not getting good grades improved significantly after they moved to a Studio School.

6 Mulgan says Studio Schools are based on a simple idea that turns education on its head. They put teamwork and practical projects at the heart of learning. This simple idea is spreading. From just one school in 2010, Studio Schools had grown to more than 40 by 2014.

---

curriculum: *n.* the content and skills taught in a school or college course

tangible: *adj.* easy to see or recognize

apprentice: *n.* a person who is trained by an expert in a job skill

fund-raiser: *n.* a person who collects money for a charity or other organization

THE DA VINCI STUDIO SCHOOL OF SCIENCE AND TECHNOLOGY

Dress Black suit, black shoes, blue "Da Vinci" shirt

Academic studies Same as traditional schools, including English, math, science

Typical work placements sales apprentice at Ford, assistant at jewelry store, fund-raiser at local charity store

Time spent at work placement
Under 16: one day every two weeks; Over 16: two days a week, paid

Homework None; all work done in school hours

Other Personal coach available all year

Location Stevenage, England

Size 300 students

Ages 14–19

Hours 9:00–5:00

A teacher writes on the board in a classroom in Aguas Calientes, Peru.

Developing Reading Skills

GETTING THE MAIN IDEAS

Use the information from the passage on pages 66–68 to answer each question.

1. How does the writer describe the approach to learning in traditional schools?

   _____

   _____

   _____

2. What is the main reason some students aren't engaged in traditional schools?

   a. They don't do well at tests.

   b. They don't see the connection to their future lives.

   c. They like doing projects.

3. Why were Studio Schools created?

   a. Too many teenagers were fighting at traditional schools.

   b. Traditional schools weren't meeting the needs of all students.

   c. There were not enough traditional schools for all students.

4. How might Geoff Mulgan describe Studio Schools? Complete the sentence.

   Studio Schools combine _____

   with _____.

SUPPORTING IDEAS WITH EVIDENCE

Scan the passage and infographics on pages 66–68, and write answers to the questions below.

1. What percentage of U.S. high school students don't feel engaged with their studies, according to a recent poll? _____

2. How many learners do not finish their education in the U.K.? _____

3. How many students are in a typical Studio School? _____

4. In Studio Schools, how much of the curriculum is covered outside the classroom? _____

5. How many Studio Schools were there in 2014? _____

FINDING SIMILARITIES AND DIFFERENCES

How are Studio Schools the same as and different from traditional schools? Use the information below (a–j) to complete the Venn diagram.

a. academic learning

b. emphasis on teamwork

c. include elementary school students

d. focus on taking tests

e. homework

f. learning is mostly project-based

g. personal coaches

h. publicly funded

i. emphasis on work placements

j. majority of time spent in a classroom

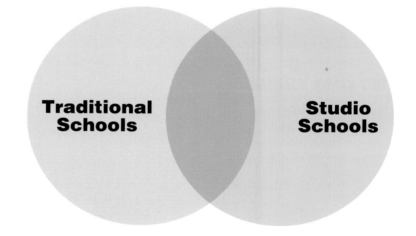

GETTING MEANING FROM CONTEXT

What do you think Geoff Mulgan means when he says that a Studio School "turns education on its head"? Discuss your ideas with a partner.

_____

_____

CRITICAL THINKING

1. Personalizing. Would you like to go to a Studio School? Why, or why not?

2. Reflecting. Mulgan says that large numbers of teenagers "learn best in teams, and they learn best by doing things for real." Do you agree with him? Explain why, or why not.

BUILDING VOCABULARY

A. **Complete the paragraph with the correct words.**

approach	determined	engage	indicated	relevant

Why do some students drop out of school? Why do some feel it is not _____ to

their lives? There are plenty of theories, ranging from poor teachers to bad curricula.

However, Rita Pierson, a teacher in the United States for more than 40 years, suggested

we take a different _____ to this question. Her experience _____ that we

should focus more on the human connection. In other words, we should look at how

teachers _____ with their students. Even simple things, she said, like

encouraging students when they fail and being _____ to understand their

problems, can make a big difference in a student's life.

B. **Choose the best option to answer each question.**

1. Which of these words best describe something that shows signs of future success?

   a. engaging   **b.** promising   **c.** surprising

2. Which of these verbs best describes joining two or more things together?

   a. create   **b.** determine   **c.** combine

3. Who or what is trained to give advice or instruction?

   a. a coach   **b.** an approach   **c.** a child

EXPLORE MORE

Find out more about Studio Schools. Go to TED.com and watch Mulgan's TED Talk called "A short intro to the Studio School." Why did Mulgan choose "Studio School" as a name for this type of school? Share your opinions of Mulgan's talk with your class.

TEDTALKS

THE KEY TO SUCCESS? GRIT

ANGELA LEE DUCKWORTH Psychologist and academic,
TED speaker

Angela Lee Duckworth wants to find out why some
students succeed where others fail.

In her late 20s, Duckworth left a job as a management consultant
to teach high school math in public schools in San Francisco,
Philadelphia, and New York. She realized that the smartest kids
were not always the ones who got the best grades.

Duckworth did some research and has proposed some new ideas
about success in learning. She thinks there is one factor that affects
students' engagement in school. She has won numerous honors
and awards for this research. In 2013, she received a Genius Grant
from the MacArthur Foundation. Her work has also generated a lot
of interest among educators.

**In this lesson, you are going to watch segments of Duckworth's
TED Talk. Use the information about Duckworth above to answer
these questions.**

1. What did Duckworth realize when she taught high school math?

    _____

2. What did her studies suggest about success in learning?

    _____

3. What was the reaction from other people to Duckworth's ideas? How
    do you know?

    _____

Duckworth's **idea worth spreading** is that the biggest predictor of success for students is not I.Q., but the ability to persevere and have passion for long-term goals.

JUST I.Q.?

PREVIEWING

Read this excerpt from Angela Lee Duckworth's talk. What surprises Duckworth about the difference between her best and worst learners? Note your answer in your own words.

❝ What struck me was that I.Q. was not the only difference between my best and my worst students. Some of my strongest performers did not have stratospheric I.Q. scores. Some of my smartest kids weren't doing so well. ❞

"What struck me . . .": "What I realized . . ."

stratospheric: *adj.* very high

I.Q.: *n.* level of someone's intelligence (an abbreviation of *intelligence quotient*)

GETTING THE MAIN IDEA

Read the excerpt below from Duckworth's talk. Then watch (▶) the first segment of Duckworth's talk. What conclusions did she come to? Check (✔) all that apply.

❝ After several more years of teaching, I came to the conclusion that what we need in education is a much better understanding of students and learning from a motivational perspective, from a psychological perspective. In education, the one thing we know how to measure best is I.Q., but what if doing well in school and in life depends on much more than your ability to learn quickly and easily? ❞

---

motivational perspective: *n.* understanding what it is that drives people to want to learn

psychological perspective: *n.* understanding how social and emotional factors affect learning

☐ 1. We need to understand more about students and learning.

☐ 2. The school curriculum is too difficult for most students.

☐ 3. It's important to look at what makes students want to learn.

☐ 4. Schools need to measure students' I.Q. more carefully.

☐ 5. Students should be trained to learn quickly and easily.

☐ 6. Schools may be putting too much focus on measuring I.Q.

CRITICAL THINKING

Predicting. **What other factors do you think Duckworth found that increase success in learning?**

TRUE GRIT

UNDERSTANDING THE OVERALL MESSAGE

Read the questions. Circle the correct answers as you watch (▶) the next segment of Duckworth's talk.

1. Which of these best describes what Duckworth means by *grit*?

    a. A very challenging situation

    b. Having good health

    c. Hard work and determination

2. Which statement best matches Duckworth's overall message?

    a. Grit is a more significant predictor of success in learning than I.Q.

    b. No one really knows why some students are more successful than others.

    c. In order to be successful learners, we must sometimes fail and start over.

UNDERSTANDING TERMS

Read the excerpt from Duckworth's talk. Then answer the questions below.

> ❝ So far, the best idea I've heard about building grit in kids is something called "growth mindset." This is an idea developed at Stanford University by Carol Dweck, and it is the belief that the ability to learn is not fixed, that it can change with your effort. Dr. Dweck has shown that when kids read and learn about the brain and how it changes and grows in response to challenge, they're much more likely to persevere when they fail, because they don't believe that failure is a permanent condition. So growth mindset is a great idea for building grit. ❯❯

---

persevere: *v.* to continue trying to achieve something even though it is difficult

permanent: *adj.* remaining the same and never changing

1. What are two effects of teaching children about "growth mindset"?

    a. They see that effort can change a person's ability to learn.

    b. They understand how the brain works.

    c. They learn that our ability to learn decreases in later life.

2. How does an understanding of "growth mindset" help learners to succeed?

    _____

SUMMARIZING THE TALK

Read the statements (a–f). Put them in the correct order in the chart to summarize Duckworth's talk.

a. Then she discovers one key factor, which she calls grit.

b. However, more work needs to be done to find out more about building grit.

c. She studies lots of learners to figure out what makes them successful.

d. "Growth mindset" may help build grit.

e. Duckworth notices that a high I.Q. doesn't always mean good grades.

f. Grit doesn't come from being naturally talented, it comes from working hard.

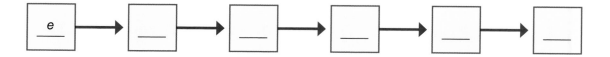

GETTING MEANING FROM CONTEXT

Duckworth says that grit is living life like it's "a marathon, not a sprint." What do you think she means by this? Discuss your ideas with a partner.

_____

_____

CRITICAL THINKING

1. Synthesizing. Duckworth and Mulgan each have ideas about why some students aren't successful in school. How are their ideas similar or different? Explain your answer.

2. Reflecting. Do you think that grit is useful in other areas of life, or does it just apply to students in school? Explain your ideas.

EXPLORE MORE

Watch Duckworth's full TED Talk at TED.com. What did her research in Chicago's public schools reveal? Share what you learned with your class.

Students work together in a village school in Burma.

A. **You are going to find out what factors people think lead to success in life. Work with a partner and follow the steps below.**

1. Brainstorm factors you think might lead to success at school or work. For example, grit, I.Q., money, or luck.

2. Ask four people you know what they think are the main factors that lead to success at school or work.

3. Report your findings to the class.

B. **As a class, discuss the most common factors that people thought led to success.**

EXPLORE MORE

In Lesson A, you learned about Rita Pierson. Watch Pierson's TED Talk "Every kid needs a champion" at TED.com. What are Pierson's ideas for improving student learning? Share what you find out with the class.

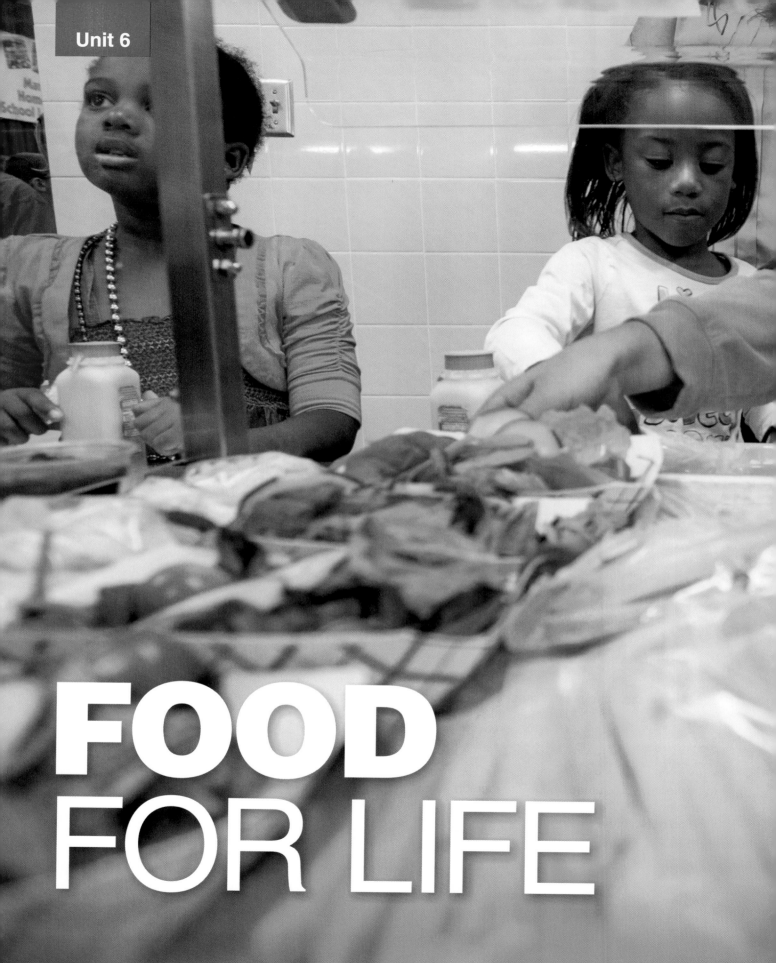

FOOD
FOR LIFE

Elementary school children choose healthy foods at a school cafeteria in Hagerstown, Maryland, U.S.A.

GOALS

IN THIS UNIT, YOU WILL:

- Read about how a celebrity chef wants people to eat better.
- Learn about problems with the food served in some schools.
- Explore ways to encourage healthy eating.

THINK AND DISCUSS

1. What kinds of foods do you like to eat? Do you think your diet is healthy?

2. What problems can people have if they eat the wrong foods?

Lesson A

PRE-READING

A. Look at the infographic on page 82 and note your answers to the questions below.

1. Which three countries are mentioned?

   _____

   _____

2. What do you think the sentence "Kids are so out of touch with what's on their plates" means?

   _____

   _____

B. Read the introduction to the reading passage on page 80. Write down your answers to the questions below. Then discuss your ideas with a partner.

1. Why do you think Huntington might be the unhealthiest place in the U.S.A.?

   _____

   _____

2. What kind of "revolution" do you think Jamie Oliver is trying to lead?

   _____

   _____

Sisters eat hamburgers at a fast-food stand in Austin, Texas, U.S.A.

In 2009, Huntington, West Virginia, was called the unhealthiest city in the United States. Jamie Oliver, a chef and activist, wanted to help—and started a food **revolution**.

1 Celebrity chef Jamie Oliver is on a mission to change people's eating habits. As part of his mission, Oliver opened a new community food center in Huntington, West Virginia, in 2009. Oliver chose Huntington largely because of the city's high rates of food-related illnesses.

FOOD REVOLUTION

At the time, over 45 percent of the adult population was obese, according to a government report. Oliver's team spent five months in Huntington coaching people about fresh food. At the food center, called Jamie's Kitchen, his team taught cooking lessons and served healthy meals. Three years after the Kitchen opened, obesity levels in Huntington had dropped by 10 percent.

NO FOOD CULTURE

2 In his books and on his TV shows, Oliver highlights why eating healthily is such a challenge today. At the heart of the issue is **widespread** ignorance. Oliver thinks many people, particularly children, are out of touch with what's on their plates. They are not aware of the ingredients in the food they eat or how it was made. At home, at school, and on Main Street, people are no longer learning about good food, cooking, and healthy eating.

3 In the past, Oliver explains, dinners at home were usually cooked with fresh ingredients. However, over the past 30 years, convenience foods have **replaced** fresh home-cooked meals. These convenience foods are highly

processed and full of additives. While these additives increase the shelf life of foods, they can be harmful to our health. Processed foods are also common in schools. Too often, the main criterion for choosing which meals to serve is cost. This means children are fed meals that are mass-produced using unhealthy ingredients.

4 Oliver also sees problems on "Main Street"— the stores and restaurants where people buy food. Fast-food restaurants offer cheap meals that are often high in sugar and fat, but low in nutrition. Additionally, the portion sizes in many restaurants are huge, encouraging people to eat more than is healthy. In supermarkets, food labeling can be confusing or misleading. For example, Oliver wonders how supermarkets can "say something is low-fat when it's full of so much sugar."

CREATING A MOVEMENT

5 Oliver has some ideas about how we can address these problems. For example, he encourages people to share simple recipes, so that more people get into the habit of home cooking. He also suggests that supermarkets hire "food ambassadors" to help **consumers** make better choices about the foods they buy. He **urges** big food brands to provide better labeling on their products. He has also worked with schools to develop healthier meals, and to help children learn about good **nutrition**.

6 Inspired by his experiences in Huntington, Oliver created an annual event called Food Revolution Day. Food Revolution Day events raise **awareness** of how food affects our well-being and remind people that cooking with fresh ingredients is fun. In 2014, groups in over 100 countries **participated**. Through initiatives like Food Revolution Day and Jamie's Kitchen, Jamie Oliver hopes people will live healthier lives. Oliver wants to create "a movement to educate every child about food [and] to inspire families to cook again."

---

processed food: *n.* packaged foods that have been prepared in order to make them last longer

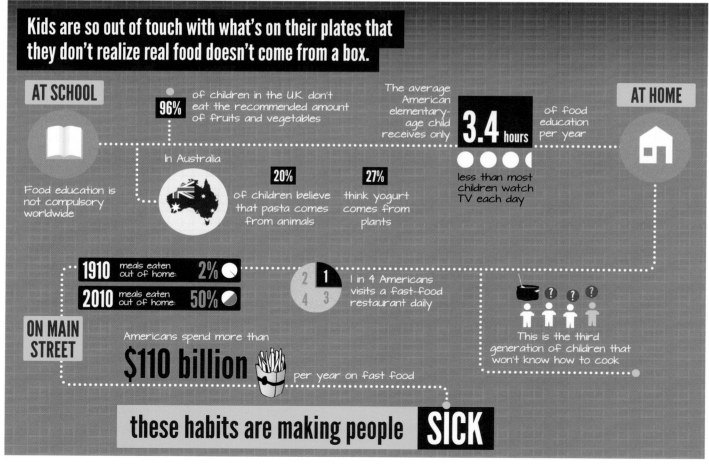

Kids are so out of touch with what's on their plates that they don't realize real food doesn't come from a box.

AT SCHOOL

96% of children in the U.K. don't eat the recommended amount of fruits and vegetables

Food education is not compulsory worldwide

In Australia

20% of children believe that pasta comes from animals

27% think yogurt comes from plants

The average American elementary-age child receives only **3.4 hours** of food education per year

less than most children watch TV each day

AT HOME

1910 meals eaten out of home: **2%**

2010 meals eaten out of home: **50%**

1 in 4 Americans visits a fast-food restaurant daily

This is the third generation of children that won't know how to cook

ON MAIN STREET

Americans spend more than **$110 billion** per year on fast food

these habits are making people **SICK**

Jamie Oliver teaches a student about healthy cooking as part of his TV show in Los Angeles, U.S.A.

Developing Reading Skills

UNDERSTANDING THE MAIN IDEAS

A. Use the information from the passage on pages 80–82. What is the reading mainly about? Choose the best answer(s).

1. How eating habits can be improved

2. How eating habits have changed in Huntington

3. Why Jamie's Kitchen was successful

B. How does Oliver want to improve people's eating habits? Write your ideas and then share them with a partner.

_____

_____

_____

IDENTIFYING PROBLEMS AND SOLUTIONS

Writers sometimes explain problems and solutions in a reading passage. These may be provided within the same paragraph, or in separate paragraphs or sections.

A. Read the passage on pages 80–82 again. Which paragraphs include examples of problems? Which paragraphs include solutions? Check (✓) the boxes.

	Problems	Solutions
Paragraph 2		
Paragraph 3		
Paragraph 4		
Paragraph 5		
Paragraph 6		

B. **Use information from the reading passage on pages 80–82 to complete this concept map.**

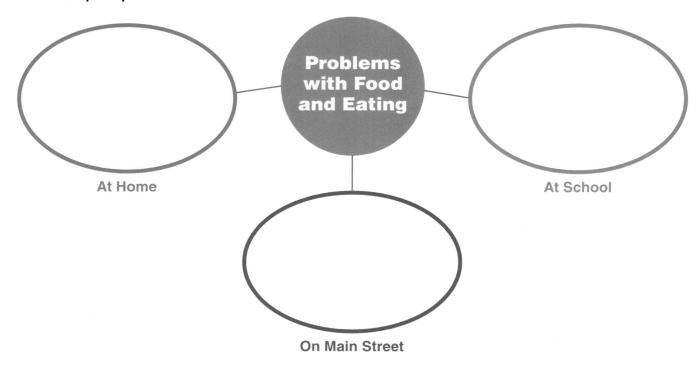

C. **What are four solutions Oliver proposes to solve some of the problems? Write your ideas and then share them with a partner.**

_____

_____

UNDERSTANDING INFOGRAPHICS

Use the infographic on page 82 to complete each sentence below.

1. Only four percent of children in the U.K. eat the recommended amount of

_____.

2. In 2010, 50 percent of all meals were eaten _____.

3. This is the third generation of children that won't _____.

4. Most children watch more hours of TV in one day than they get hours of food education in

a _____.

5. These changes at home and school are making people _____.

BUILDING VOCABULARY

A. Circle the correct word to complete each sentence.

1. For a healthier snack, **replace** / **participate** ice cream with frozen yogurt.

2. For proper **awareness** / **nutrition,** you must eat a healthy, balanced diet.

3. Health experts **urge** / **replace** people to eat less fried food.

4. As a **consumer** / **revolution,** you have a right to know what's in the food you buy.

B. Match the words (1–6) to the correct definition (a–d). Two words are extra.

_____ 1. revolution   **a.** common among many people

_____ 2. widespread   **b.** to take part in an activity or event

_____ 3. urge   **c.** a sudden or significant change in the
                                     way we live, work, or are governed

_____ 4. awareness

_____ 5. participate   **d.** an understanding of something

_____ 6. nutrition

GETTING MEANING FROM CONTEXT

A. The passage mentions that people should "get into the habit" of home cooking. What does that phrase mean? Note some ideas and discuss with a partner.

_____

_____

B. The passage states that, "Over the past 30 years, *convenience foods* have replaced fresh home-cooked meals." What are some examples of convenience foods?

_____

CRITICAL THINKING

1. Applying. How are your eating habits similar to or different from the habits mentioned in the reading passage?

2. Reflecting. Oliver wants supermarkets to hire "food ambassadors." What do you think the role of a food ambassador would be? Do you think it's a good idea?

EXPLORE MORE

Read about Oliver's Ministry of Food project in England at jamieoliver.com/jamies-ministry-of-food. Find out what people can do at each of the different centers. Share your findings with your class.

TEDTALKS

TEACH EVERY CHILD ABOUT FOOD

JAMIE OLIVER Chef and activist, TED speaker

Jamie Oliver's passion for cooking started in the kitchen of his parents' restaurant and pub. He has made over a dozen TV series and has published many bestselling cookbooks. As well as a chef, Oliver is an activist who educates people on how to eat more healthily.

In 2004, Oliver began working to improve the quality of food served at U.K. schools. In 2009, he brought a similar campaign to the United States. He recognizes that there are many other people—from health experts to lunch ladies—trying to achieve similar goals. But there are many challenges to overcome, particularly lack of funding. Oliver thinks we need to identify and thank these people and give them the resources they need.

In 2010, he was awarded the TED prize—a donation of one million dollars to make someone's wish come true. Jamie Oliver's wish is to educate people about food, and hopefully improve people's lives. "I'm not a doctor; I'm a chef," he says. "I don't have expensive equipment or medicine. I use information [and] education."

In this lesson, you are going to watch segments of Oliver's TED Talk. Use the information above to answer the questions.

1. How did Oliver get interested in cooking?

_____

Jamie Oliver's **idea worth spreading** is that we need to educate children about food, inspire families to cook, and empower people to fight obesity.

2. What main challenge do people face when trying to improve the quality of food in schools?

_____

3. What is Oliver's wish?

_____

PART 1

GUESS THE VEGETABLE

PREVIEWING

A. In the first segment of Oliver's talk, he asks schoolchildren to name particular vegetables. How well do you know these items? Match the pictures (1–6) to the correct words (a–f).

1.

2.

3.

4.

5.

6.

_____ **a.** mushroom

_____ **b.** eggplant

_____ **c.** tomato

_____ **d.** potato

_____ **e.** cauliflower

_____ **f.** beetroot

B. Read this excerpt from Oliver's talk. Which of the bold words do you think he uses?

❝ What's the **(1) problem / purpose** of school? School was always invented to arm us with the tools to make us creative, do wonderful things, make us earn a living, etc. [. . .] But we haven't really evolved it to deal with the **(2) health / hunger** catastrophes of America, OK? School food is something that most **(3) parents / kids**—31 million a day, actually—have twice a day, more than often, breakfast and lunch, 180 days of the year. So you could say that school food is quite **(4) easy / important**, really . . . ❞

---

evolved: *v.* changed and developed

catastrophe: *n.* something that causes a lot of damage; a disaster

GETTING THE MAIN IDEA

A. Watch (▶) the first segment of the talk and check your answers to the Previewing questions above.

B. What is this segment of the talk mainly about? Complete the sentences with your own ideas.

1. The problem with children not knowing the names of the vegetables is that

_____.

2. The solution Jamie Oliver suggests is

_____.

STOP THE SUGAR

PREVIEWING

Look at the photo of Jamie Oliver. Why do you think he is pushing a wheelbarrow onto the stage?

GETTING THE MAIN IDEA

In many schools in the United States, milk must be offered to children with every meal. Answer the questions with your ideas. Then check your answers as you watch (▶) the next segment of Oliver's talk.

1. What ingredients are added to the milk served in schools?

   _____

2. Why are these ingredients added?

   _____

3. How much sugar does flavored milk contain compared to a fizzy drink (soda)?

   _____

4. Does Oliver think giving milk to schoolchildren is a bad idea?

   _____

Jamie Oliver on the TED stage

CRITICAL THINKING

1. Inferring. Jamie Oliver talks about children not using cutlery. Why do you think it's a problem that kids do not use knives and forks to eat?

2. Evaluating. Do you think the wheelbarrow of sugar helped Oliver make his point? What do you think it added to his presentation?

PART 3

A NEW STANDARD

UNDERSTANDING KEY DETAILS

A. **Read the excerpt from the next segment of Oliver's talk. What key points is he making? Choose the two best statements.**

> ❝ In schools, we owe it to [children] to make sure those 180 days of the year . . . [they] need to be cooked proper, fresh food from local growers on-site. There needs to be a new standard of fresh, proper food for your children.
>
> It's profoundly important that every single American child leaves school knowing how to cook ten recipes that will save their life. That means that they can be students, young parents, and be able to sort of duck and dive around the basics of cooking, no matter what recession hits them next time. ❯❯

---

duck and dive: *idiom* to be clever enough to understand and deal with a situation

recession: *n.* a period of time when the economy of a country is doing badly

1. Schools should provide a better standard of fresh food for students.

2. Students should spend more time growing their own ingredients in school.

3. Children should all leave school knowing the same ten recipes.

4. Oliver thinks that if you can cook, you will do better during bad economic times.

B. **Now watch (▶) the rest of Oliver's talk. How would you describe his emotions during this segment of the talk? Compare your answers with a partner.**

CRITICAL THINKING

Reflecting. Oliver says that every child should know how to cook "ten recipes that will save their life." List ten meals you think are important to know how to make. What makes these ten healthy and life-saving?

Watch Oliver's full TED Talk at TED.com. How do the residents of Huntington feel about Jamie's Kitchen? Share your opinions with your class.

Project

Jamie Oliver broadcasts a live cooking class to schoolchildren across the globe as part of the third annual Food Revolution Day in 2014 in London, U.K.

A. Work with a partner. You're going to plan an event for Food Revolution Day. Choose from the following or use your own idea.

- Enroll your class in a Ministry of Food cooking class.
- Organize a trip to your local farmer's market.
- Campaign to get cooking skills on the curriculum at a school.

B. Go to the Food Revolution Day website and research your idea.

C. Design a flyer to promote the event. Include the following information.

- What is the event?
- When is it taking place?
- Who can participate?
- Why is it important to take part?

D. Post your flyer on the classroom wall, along with your classmates' flyers. With your class, discuss the following:

1. Which flyer is the best? Why?
2. What Food Revolution Day activities sound the most interesting?
3. Are you likely to join the event? Why or why not?

EXPLORE MORE

Find out about the most recent Food Revolution Day. Which events do you think were the most interesting and successful? Why? Share what you learn with your class.

BODY
SIGNS

Medalists celebrate at the 2014 Winter Olympics in Sochi, Russia.

GOALS

IN THIS UNIT, YOU WILL:

- Read about the power of nonverbal communication.
- Learn how we can use our bodies to change our attitudes.
- Explore low- and high-power poses.

THINK AND DISCUSS

1. What are some examples of body language?

2. What kinds of messages do we send through our body language?

PRE-READING

A. Look at the photo of Usain Bolt and read the caption. How do you think he feels? How do you know?

_____

_____

B. Look at the infographic on page 96. Discuss these questions with a partner.

1. Which of the poses matches the one Usain Bolt is doing?

2. What do you think the graphic tells you about how different poses make us feel?

C. Look at the title of the passage. What do you think "power poses" are?

a. How you hold your body when you win a big prize

b. How you exercise at the gym to make your body strong

c. How you sit or stand to show how powerful you are

D. Skim the passage quickly. What kind of reading passage is this? How do you know?

a. An article about some research

b. A report about a news event

c. A personal narrative

POWER POSES

1 Amy Cuddy, a social scientist and TED speaker, studies body language (or *nonverbal communication*). She is particularly interested in nonverbal expressions of power. This is what our bodies do when we are—or feel—powerful. Cuddy believes that by changing our body language, we can change how powerful we feel.

2 To **prove** this point, she ran an experiment. First, she invited a number of candidates to be interviewed for a job. Next, immediately before the interview, Cuddy asked half the candidates to practice high-power poses for two minutes. The other candidates were asked to practice low-power poses for two minutes. Then the interviews were filmed and later watched by a

Usain Bolt reacts after winning a gold medal at the 2014 Commonwealth Games in Glasgow, Scotland.

panel of interviewers who were not told what the experiment was about. The panel judged the candidates who had practiced the high-power poses very **favorably**. However, the interviewers did not want to hire anyone who had done the low-power posing.

3 Cuddy gives a simple, biological explanation for this. She says that striking some poses **releases** particular chemicals in the brain. For low-power poses, these chemicals make people believe they are powerless. Feeling powerless, they often do not **cope** well with **stress**, and they are less positive. **Conversely**, Cuddy found that high-power poses release other chemicals in the brain. These tell people that they are powerful, so they then feel **confident**. Interestingly, Cuddy

found that it didn't matter what **qualifications** a candidate had, or even what he or she actually said in the interview. "It's not about the content of the speech," explains Cuddy, "It's about the presence that they're bringing to the speech."

4 Cuddy's research suggests that doing a high-power pose for two minutes—even if we might look a bit silly when doing it—may make us feel more powerful. Feeling more powerful may very well make us *believe* we are more powerful. And that belief has the power to change our lives.

---

candidate: *n.* a person who applies for a job

presence: *n.* a way of behaving—for example, a way of standing or sitting or speaking—that makes a person memorable to others

HOW PEOPLE SEE YOU, HOW YOU SEE YOURSELF

We all know that our body language affects how people see us. But does it also shape how we see ourselves? In her TED Talk, "Your body language shapes who you are," social psychologist Amy Cuddy discusses how our posture can affect testosterone and cortisol levels in the brain and change our feelings about ourselves. That means that standing tall and proud—even when we don't feel confident—can have a positive impact on how we're perceived. So take a look in the mirror; your next success could depend on how you pose.

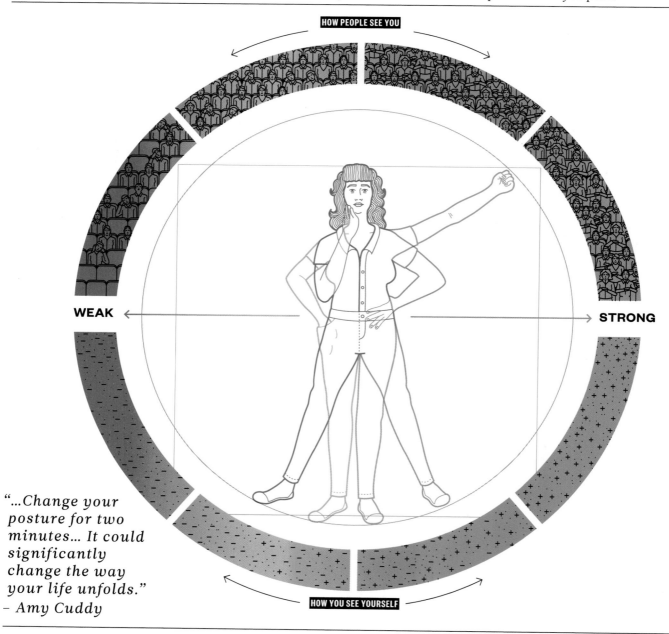

HOW PEOPLE SEE YOU

WEAK → ... → STRONG

HOW YOU SEE YOURSELF

"...Change your posture for two minutes... It could significantly change the way your life unfolds."
– Amy Cuddy

 PROTECTIVE
Placing your hand on your face or neck is a low-power pose that communicates a need for protection from other people.

 HAND-HIDING
Hiding your hands in your pockets is another example of a low-power pose; it hints that you may lack self-confidence.

 WONDER WOMAN
Shift your pose to make yourself appear bigger. That can take you from looking meek to seeming assertive.

 TALL AND PROUD
Take a private moment to hold your arms up in a V-shape and lift your chin. That can make you feel (and seem) powerful.

A swan stretches its wings. Many animals use body language to show power by "opening up" their bodies.

Developing Reading Skills

GETTING THE MAIN IDEAS

Use the information from the passage on pages 94–96 to answer each question.

1. What is the passage mostly about? Choose the best answer.

    a. Some people are naturally powerful.

    b. We can change how powerful we feel.

    c. Power makes it hard to cope with stress.

2. What did Cuddy's experiment show? Complete the sentences.

    a. Power posing can have a significant effect on

    _____

    b. After doing low-power poses,

    _____

    c. After doing high-power poses,

    _____

GETTING KEY DETAILS

A. **Choose the best word or phrase to complete each sentence below.**

    1. According to the reading passage, it **may be / may not be** possible for everyone to feel more powerful.

    2. The panel that viewed the interviews were **told / not told** about the power poses.

    3. The candidates' qualifications made **a very big difference / no difference at all** in the experiment.

    4. The results of the experiment are explained by chemicals in the **brain / muscles**.

B. **What other term does the passage use that means the same as *body language*?**

    _____

RECOGNIZING THE STRUCTURE OF A TEXT

Some expository texts explain a piece of research. These texts usually follow the same logical flow. First, the writer states the question that the researchers studied and shares the researchers' prediction about what they will find (the hypothesis). Then he describes what research was done (the method) to try to support the hypothesis. Next, he explains the results of the research and states if the hypothesis was supported or not.

A. **Match the parts of the research process with the passage excerpts below (1–4).**

conclusion   hypothesis   method   results

1. "To prove this point, she ran an experiment." _____

2. "Feeling more powerful may very well make us *believe* we are more powerful. And

that feeling has the power to change our lives." _____

3. "Cuddy believes that by changing our body language, we can change how powerful

we feel." _____

4. "[T]he panel judged the candidates who had practiced the high-power poses very

favorably." _____

B. **Using the information from the passage, complete the chart about the results of Cuddy's experiment.**

High-Power Poses	Low-Power Poses
Chemical released in brain: ▼	Chemical released in brain: ▼
Tell a person he or she is _____. ▼	Tell a person he or she is _____. ▼
Person feels _____. ▼	Person feels _____. ▼
Interviewers respond _____.	Interviewers respond _____.

BUILDING VOCABULARY

A. **Complete the text with the correct forms of the words below.**

confident	cope	release	stress

My brother, James, has to give a presentation at a conference next week. He's not a very

experienced public speaker, so he is feeling very _____ right now. But he's trying

a new strategy to _____ better with public speaking. He is practicing power

poses. By standing with his arms above his head, he _____ chemicals in his

brain. This makes him feel more _____. I hope he gives a good presentation.

B. **Match each word (1–4) with its definition (a–d).**

____ **1.** conversely   **a.** positively

____ **2.** favorably   **b.** in contrast

____ **3.** prove   **c.** skills, capabilities, or experience

____ **4.** qualifications   **d.** to show that something is true

CRITICAL THINKING

1. Analyzing. What do you think Cuddy means when she says, "It's about the presence that they're bringing to the speech"?

_____

_____

_____

2. Personalizing. Think of a famous person or someone you know in real life whose body language makes them seem powerful. What do they do specifically? How do other people react to them?

_____

_____

_____

EXPLORE MORE

There are many online resources about using body language to feel and become more successful. What kinds of nonverbal expressions can have negative effects? Share your findings with your class.

TEDTALKS

YOUR BODY LANGUAGE SHAPES WHO YOU ARE

AMY CUDDY Social psychologist and academic, TED speaker

Amy Cuddy was involved in a serious car accident when she was a student, and doctors believed she would not be able to complete college. But Cuddy prevailed, and that experience taught her a lot about persistence. Now she is a professor and social psychologist at Harvard Business School.

The challenges that Cuddy faced when she was a student have made her keenly aware of her own students' attitudes and feelings. In her classes, she observed important differences between the body language of the male and the female MBA students, and the implications those differences had on student success rates.

These observations led her to research power dynamics based on nonverbal communication—how we judge others and how we are judged without saying a word. Cuddy's work caught the public's attention. Her TED Talk on the subject has been viewed more than 20 million times.

---

prevail: *v.* to succeed against the odds

implications: *n.* possible future results or effects

Cuddy's **idea worth spreading** is that by "power posing" for two minutes, you can actually feel more powerful.

In this lesson, you are going to watch segments of Cuddy's TED Talk. Use the information about Cuddy on page 100 to answer the questions.

1. What happened to Cuddy when she was a college student?

    _____

2. What did she notice at Harvard Business School?

    _____

3. Why do you think Cuddy's TED Talk has been so popular?

    _____

PART 1

JUDGING OTHERS AND OURSELVES

PREVIEWING

A. **Read this excerpt from Cuddy's talk. Choose the statement below that provides the best summary.**

❝ So social scientists have spent a lot of time looking at the effects of our body language, or other people's body language, on judgments. And we make sweeping judgments and inferences from body language. And those judgments can really predict meaningful life outcomes, like who we hire or promote, who we ask out on a date. ❞

1. Social scientists judge people based on their body language.

2. We make judgments about one another based on our body language.

3. Businesses are hiring social scientists to help them choose their employees.

GETTING THE MAIN IDEAS

Watch (▶) the first segment of the talk and answer the questions below.

1. Why do you think Cuddy shows the photos of famous politicians? Note down some ideas and then discuss with a partner.

_____

2. What does Amy Cuddy mean by *interaction*? Choose the best definition.

   a. Talking to, or doing things with, other people

   b. The way you feel about something that was said

   c. Feeling happy about something you did or said

3. Cuddy mentions two areas of our lives on which body language can have an effect. What are they? Complete the sentences with your ideas.

   The first is _____.

   The second is _____.

4. When Cuddy talks about "the other audience" that is influenced by our nonverbal communication, who does she mean? Discuss with a partner.

CRITICAL THINKING

Reflecting. Can you think of moments in life where people may judge us based on body language? Note down your ideas and then discuss with a partner.

_____

_____

PART 2

FAKE IT TILL YOU MAKE IT?

GETTING THE MAIN POINT

A. **Read the excerpt from the next segment of Cuddy's talk. What do you think the question "Can you fake it till you make it?" means? Discuss with a partner.**

❝ So, my main collaborator, Dana Carney, who's at Berkeley, and I really wanted to know: Can you fake it till you make it? Like, can you do this just for a little while and actually experience a behavioral outcome that makes you seem more powerful? ❞

B. Watch (▶) the next segment of Cuddy's talk. Complete the sentence about Cuddy's main point.

When you pretend to be powerful, _____.

a. most people will realize you are faking

b. you are more likely to feel powerful

c. other people around you will feel powerful as well

CRITICAL THINKING

Inferring. What can we infer about risk tolerance from the results of the experiment?

_____

_____

PART 3

OUR BODIES CHANGE OUR MINDS

RECOGNIZING SEQUENCE

A. Read the statements (a–g) about Cuddy's story. As you watch (▶) the final part of the talk, put her story into the correct order (1–7).

_____ **a.** She begins graduate school at Princeton under Susan Fiske.

_____ **b.** Cuddy fakes it . . . and she makes it!

_____ **c.** Her I.Q. level drops, and she is told she won't be able to finish college.

_____ **d.** Her advisor won't allow her to quit and insists that she fake it.

_1_ **e.** Cuddy is involved in a serious car accident.

_____ **f.** Feeling she doesn't belong, she wants to quit before her first-year talk.

_____ **g.** She completes her college degree four years later than her peers.

UNDERSTANDING KEY DETAILS

A. What do you think people mean when they tell Cuddy that they don't want to feel like "a fraud" or "an impostor"? Note down your answers and then discuss your ideas with a partner.

_____

_____

B. Watch (▶) the final segment of Cuddy's talk again. Then answer the questions.

1. How did the graduate student feel before she came to talk to Cuddy?

    a. She felt that she was going to fail.

    b. She felt that she didn't belong there.

2. What did Cuddy tell the student to do?

    _____

3. What was the outcome for that student?

    _____

IDENTIFYING PURPOSE

Identifying the speaker's purpose is a good way to improve comprehension. Ask yourself questions as you listen. For example, "Why is the speaker sharing this? What does the speaker want me to understand?"

Why do you think Cuddy mentions the graduate student who came to see her? Choose the two best answers.

a. To illustrate what a supportive teacher she was

b. To reinforce the topic with an additional example

c. To prove the point about "fake it till you make it"

SUMMARIZING

Summarize the conclusion of Amy Cuddy's talk using the words below.

high-power   outcomes   power-posing   powerless

Amy Cuddy wants people to try _____ themselves, and also to share this science with others.

She especially wants it to be shared with those who feel _____. She ends the talk by reminding us that doing _____ poses for two minutes, in private, can truly change the _____ of a person's life.

CRITICAL THINKING

1. Inferring. What do you think Cuddy means when she says that the student "had actually faked it till she became it"?

    _____

    _____

    _____

2. Reasoning. Which do you think is more important, that other people believe in us or that we believe in ourselves? Give reasons for your answer.

    _____

    _____

    _____

EXPLORE MORE

Watch Amy Cuddy's full TED Talk at TED.com. In her talk, Cuddy shares several more examples that demonstrate the power of nonverbal communication. Which one was most interesting to you, and why? Share your opinions with your class.

High- and low-power poses. Can you guess which are which?

A. **Work in groups of five students. You are going to recreate Cuddy's experiment with low- and high-power poses.**

1. In your group, prepare a short presentation about Amy Cuddy's research on power posing. Or, choose a topic from another unit.
2. Choose a student to be the judge. The judge should leave the room. Two students practice a high-power pose for two minutes; the other two students practice a low-power pose.
3. Ask the judge to come back in. Each student gives his or her presentation prepared in step 1.
4. The judge decides who did a high-power pose and who did a low-power pose.

B. **As a class, discuss the results of the experiment. Use the questions below.**

- Were the judges correct?
- Did the low-power posers feel less confident?
- Did the high-power posers feel more confident?

EXPLORE MORE

Find out about the differences in nonverbal communication between various cultures. Is body language the same from culture to culture, or can you find any important differences? What are they? Share what you learn with your class.

ENERGY BUILDERS

Winds whip up clouds behind
a group of wind turbines in
Moccasin, Wyoming, U.S.A.

GOALS

IN THIS UNIT, YOU WILL:

- Read about a new way to get energy from the wind.
- Learn about someone who solved an energy problem.
- Explore other energy innovations.

THINK AND DISCUSS

1. How do you think the electricity that you use at home is generated?

2. What are some types of clean, renewable energy? Why are these types of energy sources becoming more popular?

PRE-READING

A. Do you know how we can use the wind to generate energy? Discuss your ideas with a partner.

_____

_____

B. Look at the picture on this page. Write your answers to these questions.

1. What do you think the energy kite does?

_____

_____

2. How do you think the energy kite works?

_____

_____

_____

C. Look at the infographic on page 110. What do you think the main differences are between a traditional wind turbine and the energy kite?

_____

_____

_____

KITE POWER

1 "There is incredible power in the wind," according to inventor Saul Griffith. He estimates that wind has more than enough power to provide for our global energy needs 200 times over. Now, an idea from a child's toy may help to harness this power.

2 Towering 300 feet (90 meters) above the Earth's **surface**, wind turbines are the most **visible**—and common—way to harness the power of the wind. Wind power is becoming an important **source** of energy today. Population growth means we have a greater need for energy, especially energy that does not add to global warming. According to the U.S. Department of Energy, one megawatt of wind energy can provide power for up to 400 homes without producing any carbon dioxide—a source of global warming.

3 While wind is a promising energy source, there are problems with **traditional** turbines.

The Makani team carries the energy kite prototype. Makani, founded by Saul Griffith, is a company developing airborne wind turbines.

First of all, they're expensive. This is because they're made from costly materials such as steel and fiberglass. In addition, they're only useful in places where the wind travels routinely at around 15–20 miles per hour. Only about 15 percent of land in the world has winds this strong. Turbines are already very tall, but to reach the faster wind speeds at even higher **altitudes**, they would have to be taller. But at the moment, it's not **practical** to build these taller turbines.

4 Inventor Saul Griffith got an idea from a wind-powered toy—the kite—to solve some of these problems. Griffith is developing an "energy kite," that is tethered to the ground. It flies in large circles up to 1,000 feet (300 meters) in the air. At this altitude, the wind is stronger and more **consistent** than at lower altitudes. The energy kite has blades like a regular turbine, so it **generates** electricity in a similar way.

5 Griffith's invention has some advantages over a traditional turbine. First of all, it's lighter. For example, the shaft is made of plastic, which is cheap to make. It can also generate more than twice as much wind power as a traditional turbine. Finally, because most of the energy kite is in the air, it takes up less land than a traditional turbine. It also works over water, where wind moves at even greater speeds.

6 Griffith says his invention has brought us to "the dawn of a new age of kites." He and his team are planning even bigger energy kites that could generate huge amounts of clean electricity. While he is still at the prototype stage, the early tests are promising. Griffith believes his energy kite will be an important part of the solution to our current climate and energy problems.

---

harness: *v.* to capture the power of something

airborne: *adj.* moving in the air

fiberglass: *n.* a material made from glass fibers

tether: *v.* to hold in place using a rope

HARNESSING *THE WIND*

Energy kites and traditional wind turbines generate electricity in a similar way. Wind spins the blades, which then turn a shaft. A generator behind the blades turns this movement into electricity. But, because there is no tower holding it in place, the energy kite has significant advantages. First, it uses 90 percent fewer materials and is half the cost of traditional wind turbines. Also, tethering the kite allows it to reach wind at higher altitudes in more places in the world.

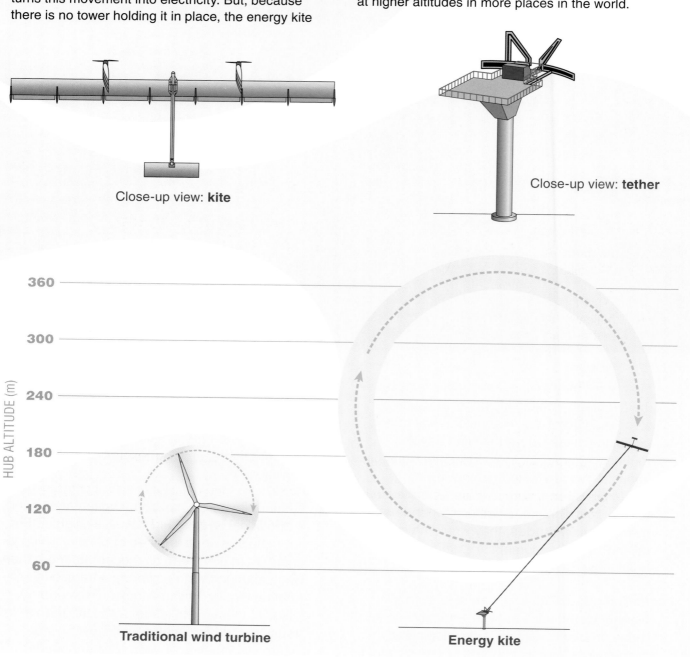

Close-up view: **kite**

Close-up view: **tether**

HUB ALTITUDE (m)

360
300
240
180
120
60

Traditional wind turbine

Energy kite

A helicopter lowers a technician to maintain a wind turbine in Denmark.

Developing Reading Skills

GETTING THE MAIN IDEAS

What are the main ideas of the passage? Write T (True) or F (False). Then correct the false statements.

_____ 1. Traditional wind turbines reach stronger winds than the energy kite.

_____ 2. A new way to harness the wind's power works like a kite.

_____ 3. The energy kite has several advantages over traditional turbines.

_____ 4. The energy kite is still in the prototype stage.

_____ 5. Energy kites use more materials, but are half the cost of traditional wind turbines.

SCANNING FOR SPECIFIC INFORMATION

Scanning involves moving your eyes quickly over a text. Scanning helps you locate specific information. It's especially useful for finding numerical information. When you scan for numbers, look for key words that appear such as _feet_, _meters_, and _percent_.

Scan the passage and infographic on pages 108–110 to find the answers to these questions.

1. How much wind power is needed to power up to 400 homes? _____ megawatt(s)

2. How much of the world has winds strong enough to power traditional wind turbines? _____ percent

3. How tall are traditional turbines? _____ feet

4. How high does the energy kite fly? _____ feet

BUILDING VOCABULARY

A. Read the paragraph. Then match each bolded word with a definition.

Wind provides a clean and easy-to-harness power **source**. In fact, Saul Griffith estimates that wind can **generate** enough electricity to power the entire world. However, there are some problems with **traditional** wind turbines. Traditional turbines are grouped in large arrangements, across hills, **visible** from people's houses. As a result, some people complain that turbines ruin the look of the landscape. Wind turbines can also harm wildlife. Animals such as birds and bats can run into the turbines and be crushed by the blades.

1. _____: easily seen

2. _____: existing in the same way for a long time

3. _____: a place or thing that something comes from

4. _____: to produce, create

B. Complete the sentences with the words below.

altitudes	consistent	practical	surface

1. At higher _____, wind speeds are significantly faster.

2. To work well, a wind turbine requires a(n) _____ wind speed of 15–20 mph. If the wind slows down, the generator will not produce enough energy.

3. Wind speeds are slow on the _____ of the Earth. Faster wind speeds occur several hundred feet above the ground.

4. It's not _____ to use wind power in places where wind speeds are not fast. In places like these, solar power can be a better alternative.

MAKING COMPARISONS

What are the differences between a traditional turbine and the energy kite? Complete the sentences using the words below.

altitude	blades	shaft	tether

1. Both the traditional turbine and the energy kite have _____, a _____, and a generator.

2. An energy kite has a _____, but a traditional turbine does not.

3. The energy kite reaches a higher _____ than a traditional turbine does.

GETTING MEANING FROM CONTEXT

Some verbs combine with certain prepositions. It's a good idea to memorize these combinations.

Find the underlined verb + preposition combinations in paragraph 5 on page 109. Then choose the correct meaning for each.

1. The energy kite flies in the air, so it <u>takes up</u> less land than a traditional turbine does.

    a. destroys   **b.** uses   **c.** has

2. The shaft on an energy kite is <u>made of</u> plastic, which is much lighter than steel.

    a. created from   **b.** similar to   **c.** used with

CRITICAL THINKING

1. Evaluating. Why do you think some people might not like the energy kite as an energy solution?

2. Reflecting. Is wind an appropriate source of power where you live? Why, or why not?

EXPLORE MORE

Learn more about Saul Griffith's energy kite invention. Watch his TED Talk "High-altitude wind energy from kites!" at TED.com. Find out some ways that people used kites for power in the past. Share your information with the class.

The Makani team with a prototype of the energy kite.

TEDTALKS

HOW I HARNESSED THE WIND

WILLIAM KAMKWAMBA Inventor, TED speaker

🔊 A born inventor, William Kamkwamba saved his family with one of his inventions when he was just 14 years old.

Kamkwamba grew up in a poor farming family in Malawi. His family grew maize, like most Malawian farmers. In 2001, the country experienced a terrible famine causing many Malawians to starve. Kamkwamba's family ate one meal per day, at night, and the only food they ate was a small amount of *nsima*—cornmeal paste.

But Kamkwamba worked out a way to help his family. He invented a simple machine that helped his family grow more food. His invention also helped everyone in his community. News about his invention got Kamkwamba a lot of attention. As a result, people from around the world donated money and other kinds of help to improve life in his village.

---

maize: *n.* corn   **famine:** *n.* a serious lack of food

In this lesson, you are going to watch segments of Kamkwamba's TED Talk. Use the information about Kamkwamba above to answer the questions.

1. Where is William Kamkwamba from?

   _____

2. What happened in Kamkwamba's country in 2001?

   _____

3. What were two results of Kamkwamba's invention?

   _____

   _____

Kamkwamba's **idea worth spreading** is that resourcefulness, knowledge, and purpose can create change in a community even in the absence of a formal education or money.

PART 1

CHALLENGES IN MALAWI

PREVIEWING

Read this excerpt from William Kamkwamba's talk. What words do you think are missing? Share your ideas with a partner. Then watch (▶) the first segment of the talk and check your answers.

« In Malawi, the secondary school, you have to pay school fees. Because of the hunger,

I was forced to _____ school. I looked at my father and looked at those dry fields.

It was the future I couldn't accept.

I felt very happy to be at the secondary school, so I was determined to do anything possible

to _____ education. So I went to a library. I _____ books, science books,

especially physics. I couldn't read English that well. I used diagrams and pictures to

_____ the words around them. »

RECOGNIZING MAIN POINTS

Work with a partner. Discuss your answers to these questions.

1. What problem did Kamkwamba want to solve?

2. What first step did he take to try to solve the problem?

UNDERSTANDING CAUSES AND EFFECTS

Complete the flowchart by putting the events (a–f) in the right order.

a. Kamkwamba studied science books.

b. Kamkwamba's family had no money and was very hungry.

c. Kamkwamba learned by studying diagrams and pictures.

d. There was a famine in Malawi.

e. Kamkwamba went to the library to learn.

f. Kamkwamba could not go to school to continue his education.

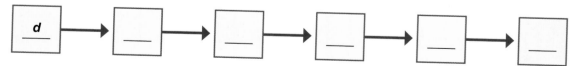

CRITICAL THINKING

Inferring. Why do you think Kamkwamba tells the audience about his past speaking experience?

PART 2

A WIND-BASED SOLUTION

PREVIEWING

A. **Scan the following excerpt from Kamkwamba's talk. Then discuss the questions below with a partner.**

>> Another book put that knowledge in my hands. It said a windmill could pump water and generate electricity. Pump water meant irrigation, a defense against hunger, which we were experiencing by that time. So I decided I would build one windmill for myself. But I didn't have materials to use, so I went to a scrap yard where I found my materials. Many people, including my mother, said I was crazy. >>

irrigation: *n.* supplying land with water so plants will grow

scrap yard: *n.* a place where people leave leftover building materials, such as wood or metal

1. Why did Kamkwamba decide to build a windmill?

2. What materials from the scrap yard do you think he used to build his windmill?

B. **Watch (▶) the next part of Kamkwamba's TED Talk. Look back at your ideas in Exercise A. Were your answers correct?**

William Kamkwamba's cousin, Gift, climbs one of the windmills they built.

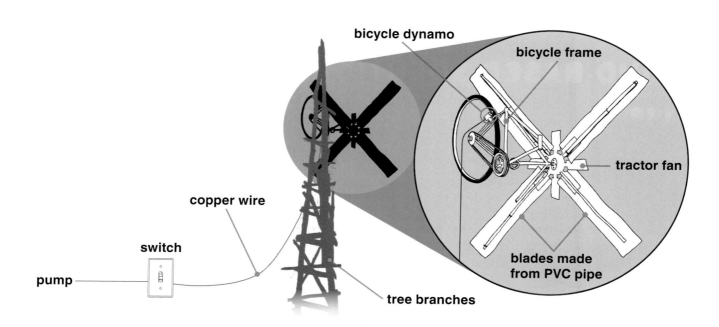

VISUALIZING A PROCESS

A. Look at the diagram of Kamkwamba's windmill. What materials do you think he found in the scrap yard? Which materials do you think he found in the fields? Discuss with a partner.

B. How does Kamkwamba's windmill work? Put the steps in the correct order. Number them from 1 to 5.

_____ The pump pumps water.

__1__ Wind moves the PVC blades of the windmill.

_____ The switch controls a pump.

_____ The movement of the blades powers a dynamo which generates electricity.

_____ Electricity travels down a copper wire to a switch.

CRITICAL THINKING

Synthesizing. How is Kamkwamba's innovation similar to and different from Jane Chen's idea from Unit 3? What do you think these two people have in common?

EXPLORE MORE

Find out more about Kamkwamba's windmill. Watch his other TED Talk called "How I built a windmill" at TED.com. How did Kamkwamba's experience affect him? How is his life different today? Share your information with the class.

Project

Taylor Wilson, a nuclear physicist, built a nuclear reactor at age 14.

A. You are going to find out about other innovative solutions to energy problems. Work with a partner. Go to TED.com and view the following TED Talks.

- Taylor Wilson: *Yup, I built a nuclear fusion reactor*
- Donald Sadoway: *The missing link to renewable energy*
- Justin Hall-Tipping: *Freeing energy from the grid*

B. Choose one of the talks. With your partner, answer the following questions.

- Who is the person giving the talk? What is his/her background?
- What motivated this person to invent something? What problem did he/she want to solve?
- What is his/her innovation? What materials is it made from? How does it work?

C. Use your answers to create a two-minute presentation. You can use diagrams, photos, and video to explain your information.

D. Work with two other pairs and follow the steps below.

1. Give your presentations.
2. As you listen, take notes.
3. At the end, review your notes. Which TED speaker is the most interesting to you? Why?

EXPLORE MORE

Learn more about interesting inventions. Go to TED.com and watch Saul Griffith's TED Talk "Everyday inventions." Share what you learn with your class.

CHANGING
PERSPECTIVES

Artist Sue Austin performs "Creating the Spectacle" in the Red Sea. Austin is changing people's perspectives about wheelchairs.

GOALS

IN THIS UNIT, YOU WILL:

- Read about someone who thinks in pictures.
- Learn about someone who challenges the way people think about her disability.
- Explore how disability contributes to people's experiences.

THINK AND DISCUSS

1. Look at the photo. How do you think this person feels?

2. What surprises you about the photo?

PRE-READING

A. Autism (sometimes called autism spectrum disorder, or ASD) affects how someone experiences and interacts with the world. What do you know about autism? Discuss with a partner.

B. Look at the photo and skim the first two paragraphs on this page. What do you think this passage is mostly about?

   a. A woman who studies the challenges of certain disabilities

   b. A woman who teaches people about her disability

   c. A woman who has turned her disability into an advantage

C. Write your answers to the questions below.

   1. What possible challenges might people face when working with animals?

   _____

   _____

   2. What personal qualities do you think a person should have to work well with animals?

   _____

   _____

Temple Grandin designs plans for livestock farms that reduce the fear that cattle may experience.

1 Temple Grandin is an expert in animal behavior. She also has autism. Some people view autism as a very limiting disability, but Grandin disagrees. She believes that if there were no autism in the world, we would "still be socializing in front of a wood fire at the entrance to a cave." Why? Grandin thinks that some people with autism have brains that can solve problems "normal" brains cannot.

2 No one knows for sure what causes autism, but scientists believe it begins during the very early stages of brain development. Autism exists on a spectrum—from very **severe** to moderate—and it **affects** people in different ways. Often, people with autism have trouble socializing and communicating normally with

THINKING IN PICTURES

We often make incorrect assumptions about people when we meet them for the first time. This may be especially true when that person has a disability or an illness. Temple Grandin challenges these assumptions.

other people. For Grandin, autism also affects the way she thinks and understands the world.

VISUAL THINKER

3 Grandin, like many people with autism, is a visual thinker—"I think in pictures, not in language," she says. For example, if you ask most people to think of a shoe, they might "see" in their mind one or two shoes. Grandin, however, remembers all the **specific** shoes that she knows and visualizes them in her mind. She says that her mind "works like Google Images." Like Google, she can very quickly categorize the images and **arrange** them in a specific order. She can also "animate" the images and make them into little movies.

4 This ability to think **visually** has helped Grandin in her career. For example, she has a unique understanding of how cattle think. According to animal researchers, cattle think in pictures, not language—similar to how Grandin's mind works. With this insight, she was able to design plans for livestock farms that reduce the fear that cattle may experience. For example, cattle are easily distracted and worried by things like waving flags or even a hose on the ground. Grandin's designs take away those visual distractions, resulting in calmer livestock.

5 Grandin's visual thinking means she can also picture how her designs might work. She creates a mental **simulation** of her designs and does a test run of the equipment in her

mind. She says that the "normal brain **ignores** the details," but her brain looks at every tiny aspect of the design. She makes sure the system works even before it's built.

6 According to Grandin, an autistic mind is "a specialist mind—good at one thing, bad at something else." Her autism has made her an expert in animal **welfare**. She believes that other people with autism may be able to solve global problems or invent some incredible software. As she points out, "the world needs all kinds of minds."

---

assumptions: *n.* things that you believe are true even though you have no proof

spectrum: *n.* a range of qualities, situations, etc.

distracted: *adj.* not concentrating on something because you are thinking about something else

AUTISM SPECTRUM

Autism Spectrum Disorder (ASD) affects individuals in different ways and can range from very mild to severe.

ASD is a neurological condition that affects the way a person experiences and interacts with the world.

delayed & disordered language

impaired social interaction

repetitive behavior

restricted range of interest

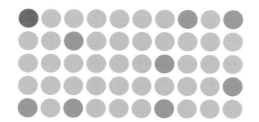

1 *in* 50 KIDS HAVE **ASD** IN THE U.S.

BOYS ARE 4x MORE LIKELY TO HAVE **ASD**

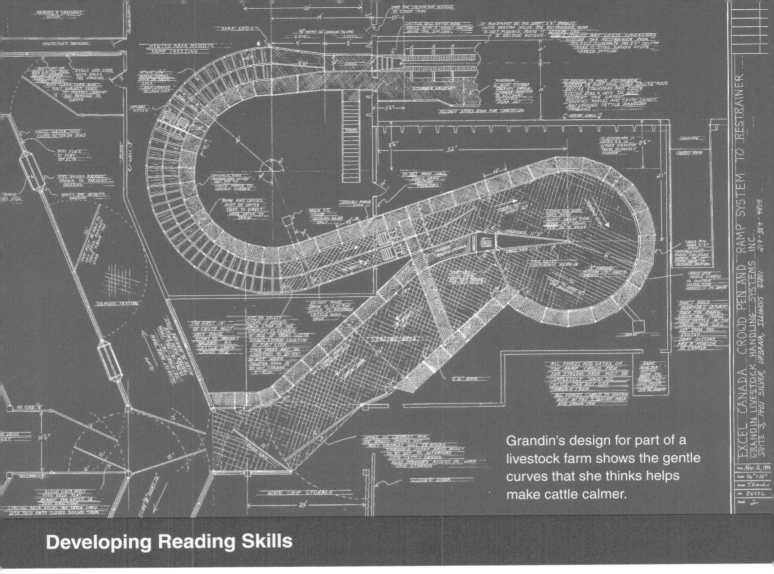

Grandin's design for part of a livestock farm shows the gentle curves that she thinks helps make cattle calmer.

Developing Reading Skills

SCANNING FOR INFORMATION

Answer the questions below about the passage and infographic on pages 122–124.

1. What causes autism?

   _____

2. According to scientists, when does autism begin?

   _____

3. Who is more likely to have autism, boys or girls?

   _____

4. What are three effects of autism?

   _____

   _____

   _____

GETTING THE MAIN IDEAS

Use information from the passage on pages 122–124 to answer each question.

1. What does Temple Grandin do?

    a. She works with animals.

    b. She works with autistic children.

    c. She is a farmer.

2. What does Temple Grandin say about autism?

    a. Autism makes a person good at a lot of different things.

    b. People with autism have specialized skills.

    c. We have to find a cure for autism.

3. According to Grandin, how does her autism help her in her job? Complete the sentence.

    Autism lets Grandin _____.

    a. avoid using language to communicate

    b. think in pictures in a similar way to animals

    c. talk more easily to animals

UNDERSTANDING KEY DETAILS

Grandin describes herself as a visual thinker. Complete the chart with three things her mind is able to do according to the passage on pages 122–124.

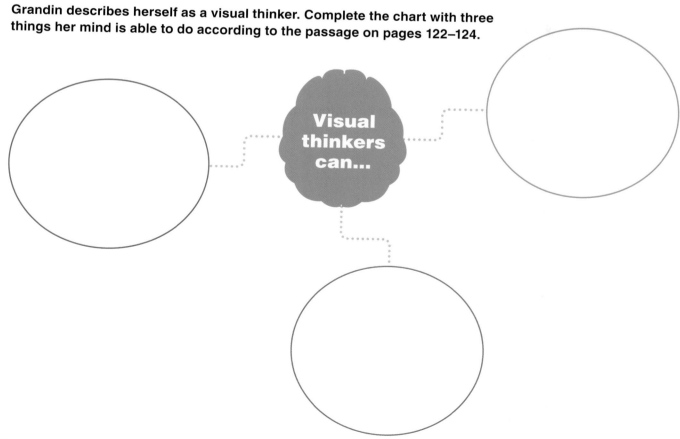

Visual thinkers can...

BUILDING VOCABULARY

A. **Complete the paragraph using the words below.**

affect	visually	simulations	welfare

Temple Grandin understands how simple things like dark shadows and waving flags

_____ animals. When she designs her systems for farms and cattle-processing

plants, she works hard to ensure that animals don't see or encounter things that will make

them feel afraid. Grandin can visualize her plans in her mind. These mental _____

help her understand how her systems might work. Due to her ability to think _____

and understand animals, Grandin has important insights into animal _____.

B. **For each bold word, choose the word or phrase that is closer in meaning.**

1. **ignore**

   a. notice   **b.** pay no attention to

2. **arrange**

   a. sort   **b.** understand

3. **specific**

   a. general   **b.** particular

4. **severe**

   a. strong   **b.** moderate

GETTING MEANING FROM CONTEXT

According to the passage, Grandin does a "test run" of her designs in her mind. What is a test run? Do you ever do test runs of things in your mind? Note some examples.

_____

_____

CRITICAL THINKING

1. Inferring. Grandin believes that if there were no autism in the world, we would "still be socializing in front of a wood fire at the entrance to a cave." What do you think she means by this?

   _____

2. Reflecting. How do you think Grandin's story might help change people's perceptions of autism? Discuss with a partner.

EXPLORE MORE

Watch Temple Grandin's TED Talk called "The world needs all kinds of minds" at TED.com. What other things did you learn about autism that surprised you? Share what you learned with the class.

TEDTALKS

DEEP SEA DIVING . . . IN A WHEELCHAIR

SUE AUSTIN Performance artist, TED speaker

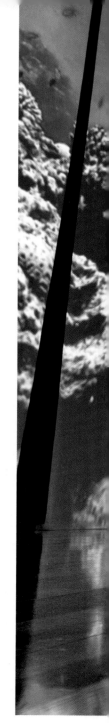

When artist Sue Austin was a young woman, a serious illness forced her to start using a wheelchair.

When she began using the wheelchair, she noticed that some people behaved differently toward her. She felt they saw her mainly as a person with limited mobility, without taking the time to appreciate her abilities and interests. Today, she creates art to try to change people's preconceptions about disabilities.

One way that Austin changes people's ideas is through an artistic organization called Freewheeling. In one project, Austin put paint on the wheels of her wheelchair and drew lines on the sidewalk. These loops and wavy lines show the freedom that her wheelchair gives her.

---

preconceptions: *n.* opinions that people form about something before they have a lot of information about it

In this lesson, you are going to watch segments of Austin's TED Talk. Use the information above to answer the questions.

1. Why did Sue Austin begin using a wheelchair?

_____

_____

Sue Austin's **idea worth spreading** is that a wheelchair doesn't have to mean "disability." It can be a new way to see and experience the world.

2. How did people behave toward Austin when she started using the wheelchair?

   _____

   _____

3. How do you think Austin's project with Freewheeling can change the way people see disabilities?

   _____

   _____

Sue Austin doing "freewheeling" art

PART 1

CHANGING IDENTITIES

PREVIEWING

A. **Read the excerpt below from Sue Austin's talk. Complete the excerpt with your own ideas. Then share your ideas with a partner.**

❮❮ When I started using the wheelchair, it was a tremendous _____. I'd seen

my life slip away and become restricted. It was like having an enormous new

_____ . . . But even though I had this newfound joy and freedom, people's

reaction completely _____ towards me. It was as if they couldn't see me

anymore, as if an invisibility cloak had descended. They seemed to _____ me in

terms of their assumptions of what it must be like to be in a wheelchair. ❯❯

---

tremendous: *adj.* extremely good

invisibility cloak: *n.* a cape that covers a person and makes it impossible for other people to see him or her

B. **How do you think Austin felt when she started using the wheelchair? Discuss with a partner.**

GETTING THE MAIN IDEA

A. Watch (▶) the first segment of Austin's TED Talk and check your answers to the Previewing activities.

B. Read the excerpt below from Austin's talk and then answer the question.

❝ When I asked people their associations with the wheelchair, they used words like *limitation, fear, pity,* and *restriction.* I realized I'd internalized these responses and it had changed who I was on a core level. A part of me had become alienated from myself. I was seeing myself not from my perspective, but vividly and continuously from the perspective of other people's responses to me. ❞

internalize: *v.* to make a belief or value part of your way of thinking

alienate: *v.* to make a person feel like he or she is no longer part of a whole

How did Austin respond to people's reactions?

CRITICAL THINKING

Inferring. Austin says that she wants to "reclaim her identity." What does she mean by this? Discuss with a partner.

PART 2

AN AMAZING JOURNEY

UNDERSTANDING MAIN IDEAS

A. Watch (▶) the next segment of Austin's talk. Write four words or phrases that describe how you feel when you watch her underwater dive.

B. Complete the sentences about Austin.

1. Austin expresses the _____ that she feels in her wheelchair.

    a. joy and freedom

    b. creativity and curiosity

    c. satisfaction and relief

2. According to Austin, when people see her underwater in her wheelchair, they _____.

    a. feel surprised or confused

    b. feel nervous for her

    c. feel the same way she does

RECOGNIZING TONE AND MESSAGE

Read the excerpt from Austin's talk. Then answer the questions below.

> It is the most amazing experience, beyond most other things I've experienced in life. I literally have the freedom to move in 360 degrees of space and an ecstatic experience of joy and freedom. And the incredibly unexpected thing is that other people seem to see and feel that, too . . .
>
> And I'm thinking, it's because in that moment . . . they have to think in a completely new way. And I think that moment of completely new thought perhaps creates a freedom that spreads to the rest of other people's lives. For me, this means that they're seeing the value of difference, the joy it brings when, instead of focusing on loss or limitation, we see and discover the power and joy of seeing the world from exciting new perspectives. »

1. Why does Austin think people's reactions to her wheelchair changed?

   _____

2. Which two statements do you think best match Austin's overall message? Discuss with a partner.

   a. People with disabilities face challenges that most people are not aware of.

   b. People should value their differences and not see just limitations and restrictions.

   c. Seeing or experiencing something for the first time can create a sense of freedom.

CRITICAL THINKING

Comparing. What perceptions did Temple Grandin and Sue Austin want to change? What did Grandin and Austin do to change people's perceptions?

EXPLORE MORE

Look at more pictures of Sue Austin's work on the TED Blog at TED.com. Watch other videos of her wheelchair dives. Share what you liked with your class.

Project

Huang Guofu paints at an art studio in Chongqing City, China. Huang, a physically disabled artist, uses paintbrushes held in his mouth and foot.

A. Work with a partner. You are going to research another person whose accomplishments challenge our preconceptions about disability. Choose one of the people below or choose your own person to research, and answer the questions.

- Sudha Chandran
- Lenín Moreno
- Stephen Hawking
- Huang Guofu

1. What is the person's "disability"?

2. What are this person's accomplishments or talents?

3. How is the person's "disability" a challenge?

4. How is the "disability" a strength?

B. Use your information to create a two-minute presentation. You can use maps, photos, and video to explain your information.

C. Give your presentations. Which person would you most like to talk with and why? What questions would you ask him or her?

EXPLORE MORE

Watch a TED Talk by Stella Young, Aimee Mullins, Chris Downey, or Maysoon Zayid. How is their perspective on disability similar to or different from the views shared by Grandin and Austin?

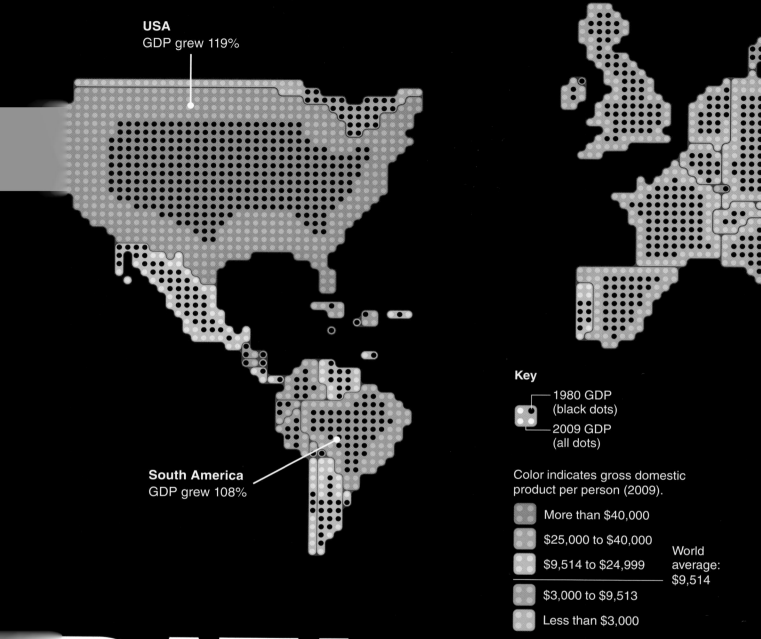

USA
GDP grew 119%

South America
GDP grew 108%

Key
1980 GDP
(black dots)
2009 GDP
(all dots)

Color indicates gross domestic
product per person (2009).

More than $40,000

$25,000 to $40,000

$9,514 to $24,999

World
average:
$9,514

$3,000 to $9,513

Less than $3,000

DATA
DETECTIVES

Many analysts use gross domestic product (GDP) as a way of assessing a country's economic performance. GDP is the amount of goods and services that a country's businesses, residents, and government produce in one year. In this map, each country is sized according to its GDP rather than its physical area.

China
GDP grew 1,506%

Japan
GDP grew 74%

Africa
GDP grew 151%

GOALS

IN THIS UNIT, YOU WILL:

- Read about someone who works with data.
- Learn about the benefits of visual data.
- Explore your own social data.

THINK AND DISCUSS

1. Look at the map. What does it show? Read the caption to check your answer.

2. What are the advantages of showing data in this way?

135

PRE-READING

A. **What does the infographic on these pages show? Choose the best three answers.**

    1. Selected cities' heights above sea level

    2. Predicted height of sea levels over time

    3. When selected cities will be below sea level

    4. Why ice sheets are getting smaller and sea levels are rising

B. **What message, or story, does this infographic tell? Write your ideas and then discuss with a partner.**

    _____

    _____

    _____

C. **Look at the Venn diagram and caption on page 138. Do you think the "When Sea Levels Attack!" infographic is an example of effective information design? Why or why not? Discuss with a partner.**

D. **Read the introductory paragraph on page 137. Why do you think David McCandless thinks information is beautiful? Discuss your ideas with a partner.**

years	sea level
8000	80m

When Sea Levels Attack!
How long have we got?

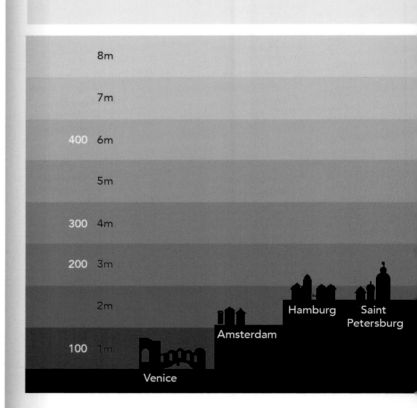

1000	20m

	8m
	7m
400	6m
	5m
300	4m
200	3m
	2m
100	1m

Hamburg   Saint Petersburg

Amsterdam

Venice

Note: Heights above sea level vary across cities. Lowest points used.

Source: IPCC, NASA, Realclimate.org, NewScientist.com, Potsdam Institute, Sea Level Explorer

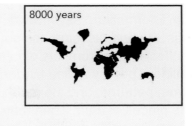

8000 years

Antarctic ice sheet
(South Pole)
73m

Greenland ice sheet
6.5m

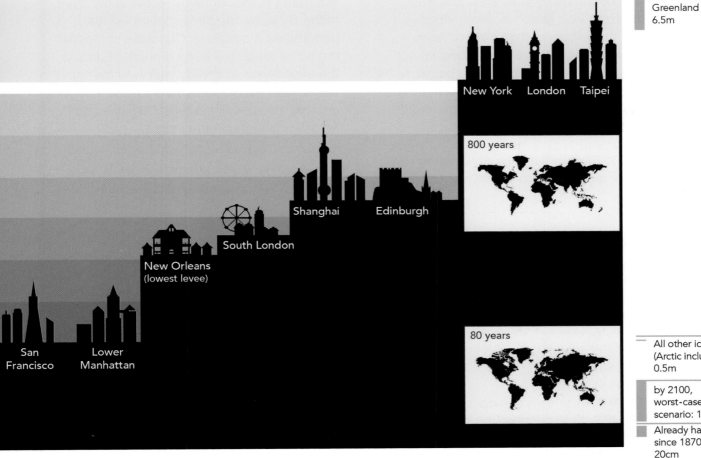

New York   London   Taipei

800 years

Shanghai   Edinburgh

South London

New Orleans
(lowest levee)

San
Francisco

Lower
Manhattan

80 years

All other ice
(Arctic included)
0.5m

by 2100,
worst-case
scenario: 1m

Already happened
since 1870
20cm

INFORMATION IS BEAUTIFUL

With the vast amount of data available today, some of us may be suffering from data glut. Journalist David McCandless thinks that the solution lies in well-designed visuals that can help us make sense of a **complex** world.

1 "There's something almost quite **magical** about visual information," says David McCandless. He and his team use software to scrape—collect—data from lots of different sources online. They try to find hidden **connections**, patterns, and stories that connect the pieces of data. Then they **create** infographics that people might find interesting and useful. Also, as McCandless says, infographics can "just look cool!"

2 For example, a world map usually represents the size of countries by land area. But what does the world look like if we see nations according to their population size, or how much they **consume**? This kind of visual not only helps us understand the world better; it can also change our perspective about it. By connecting different data, we can get a more complete picture of the world.

3 According to McCandless, by **visualizing** information, we turn it into a landscape that we can explore with our eyes—"a sort of information map." As McCandless explains, the human eye easily notices and **appreciates** visual patterns. McCandless calls patterns the "language of the eye." On the other hand, words and numbers are the "language of the mind." McCandless believes that if you combine patterns with words and numbers, you can speak two languages at the same time, "each **enhancing** the other."

4 The solution to information overload, according to McCandless, is using our eyes more. By visualizing information, we can understand it better. McCandless compares the act of reading a large amount of data to the experience of finding your way through the wilderness. When you come across a beautiful graphic, he says, it's a relief. "It's like coming across a clearing in the jungle."

---

glut: *n.* too much of something that cannot all be used

wilderness: *n.* an area of natural land unused by people

What Makes Good Information Design?

According to David McCandless, the key components of a good information design are that the information needs to be interesting (meaningful & relevant) and have integrity (accuracy, consistency). The design also needs to have form (beauty & structure) and function (it has to work and be easy to use).

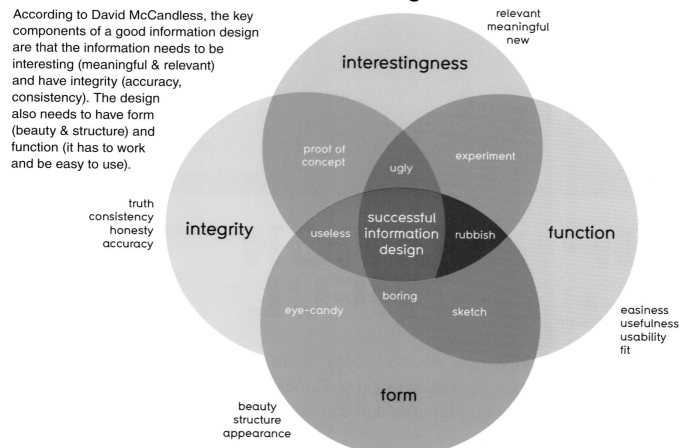

relevant
meaningful
new

interestingness

truth
consistency
honesty
accuracy

integrity

proof of concept

ugly

experiment

useless

successful information design

rubbish

function

boring

eye-candy

sketch

easiness
usefulness
usability
fit

form

beauty
structure
appearance

Developing Reading Skills

GETTING THE MAIN IDEAS

**Use information from the passage on pages 136–138 to answer each question.
Choose the best answer.**

1. What does David McCandless do?

    a. He studies visual data and explains it with words.

    b. He collects data and presents it visually.

    c. He reviews visual data for large organizations.

2. What problem does McCandless want to solve?

    a. We don't get enough data every day.

    b. We get too much data every day.

    c. We ignore online data unless it is in an infographic.

UNDERSTANDING DETAILS

A. **Why is presenting information visually useful? Choose the four ideas that are stated in the passage.**

Infographics ⸺⸺⸺.

1. can be understood by people who speak different languages

2. tell a story

3. can change our perspective

4. help us to connect different sources of data together

5. help us understand information better

6. are more entertaining to look at

7. give us a more complete picture of the world

8. take less time to read than words and numbers

B. **Look at the choices in Exercise A that are not mentioned in the reading. Do you think that these are also examples of the benefits of visual data? Discuss with a partner.**

C. **What do McCandless and his team do when they look at different sources of data? Complete each sentence.**

    a. They gather together ⸺⸺⸺⸺⸺⸺.

    b. They try to discover ⸺⸺⸺⸺⸺⸺.

    c. They produce ⸺⸺⸺⸺⸺⸺.

UNDERSTANDING INFOGRAPHICS

Many people use infographics to tell a story or explain complex information visually. Most infographics include a mixture of text, pictures, and statistics. Being able to read infographics is an important 21st-century skill.

Use information from the infographic on pages 134–135 to answer each question. Discuss your answers with a partner.

1. What do the size and color of each country represent?

2. What do the black dots and the light dots represent?

3. Circle the region whose GDP has grown the most since 1980.

    a. United States

    b. South America

    c. China

4. McCandless calls patterns the "language of the eye" and words and numbers the "language of the mind." How do you think this infographic uses both the language of the eye and the language of the mind? Discuss with a partner.

GETTING MEANING FROM CONTEXT

A. **The passage states that we are suffering from "data glut." What does this phrase mean? Write your idea and discuss with a partner.**

_____

B. **Find and circle the two-word expression in the passage that has the same meaning as *data glut*.**

BUILDING VOCABULARY

A. **Choose the word or phrase that has the closest meaning to the bolded word.**

1. **magical**

    a. difficult   b. amazing   c. complete

2. **enhancing**

    a. confusing the issue   b. changing the style   c. improving the quality

3. **consume**

    a. use   b. like   c. want

4. **complex**

    a. hard to understand   b. easy to understand   c. important to understand

B. Use the "Bandwidth of the Senses" infographic and the words below to complete the paragraph.

appreciate   **connection**   **created**   **visualize**

Danish physicist Tor Norretranders _____ this infographic to help us

_____ the power of our senses: sight, touch, smell, hearing, and taste.

Norretranders made a(n) _____ between our senses and computing equipment to

show how quickly we process information with each of our senses. Our sense of sight is

the fastest. It's like a computer network. Taste is the slowest. It processes information as

slowly as a pocket calculator. This infographic helps us better _____ how

powerful our sense of sight is in comparison with our other senses. Most importantly,

however, the tiny white section in the bottom right corner shows how much information

we are actually aware of: just 0.7 percent of what we see, smell, taste, touch, and hear.

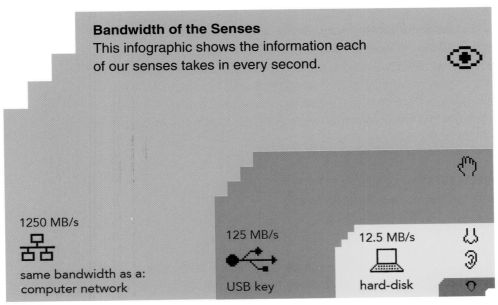

Bandwidth of the Senses
This infographic shows the information each of our senses takes in every second.

1250 MB/s
same bandwidth as a:
computer network

125 MB/s
USB key

12.5 MB/s
hard-disk

CRITICAL THINKING

1. **Inferring.** McCandless says that when you come across a beautiful graphic, "it's like coming across a clearing in the jungle." What do you think he means by this?

2. **Personalizing.** Think about how you spend a typical day. What do you do? How long do you do each thing? What kind of infographic do you think might best show this data? Make an infographic about your day and share it with a partner.

EXPLORE MORE

Go to McCandless's website, informationisbeautiful.net. Find an infographic that you think is particularly interesting and effective. Share it with your class.

TEDTALKS

THE BEAUTY OF DATA VISUALIZATION

DAVID McCANDLESS Data journalist, TED speaker

🔊 David McCandless makes infographics—simple, elegant ways to understand complex information. Surprisingly, McCandless started designing without formal instruction in art or design.

McCandless started working as a computer programmer and then wrote articles for magazines and websites for about 20 years. However, when he started designing infographics, he realized that he already knew a lot about design. As he explains, "I was sensitive to the ideas of grids and space and alignment and typography." Years of looking at media, like magazine articles and websites, gave McCandless a basic understanding of good design. His book *Information Is Beautiful* includes infographics about dozens of topics, from politics to pop music.

---

grids: *n.* patterns of straight lines that cross each other to make squares

alignment: *n.* arrangement in a straight line, or in appropriate positions

typography: *n.* the style and appearance of printed letters and words

In this lesson, you are going to watch segments from McCandless's TED Talk. Use the information above about McCandless to answer these questions.

1. Given McCandless's present job, what is surprising about his education and work experience?

   _____

2. How do you think the jobs of a journalist and an infographic designer are similar?

   _____

3. What lessons did McCandless learn about designing infographics from his previous jobs?

   _____

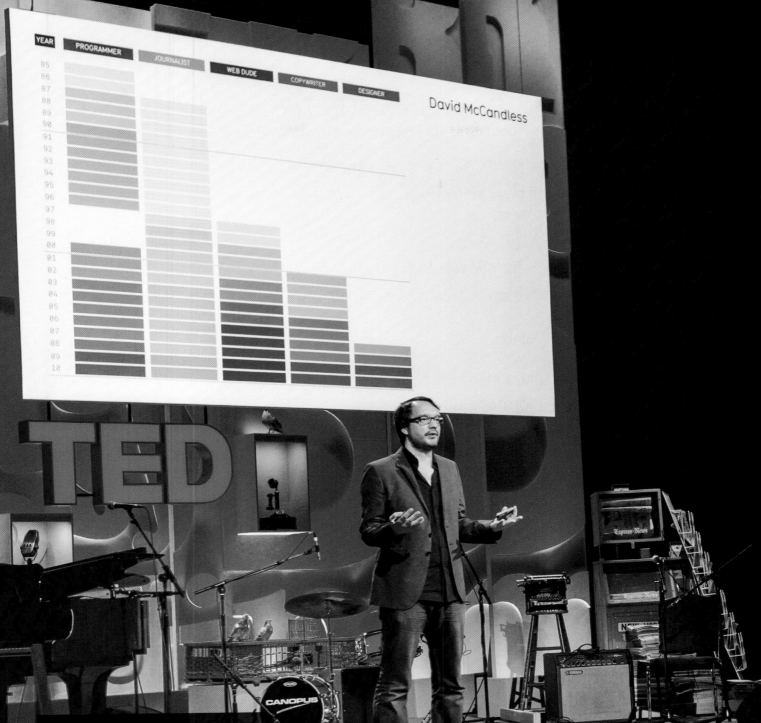

McCandless's **idea worth spreading** is that visualizing data into beautiful designs can help us understand complex information.

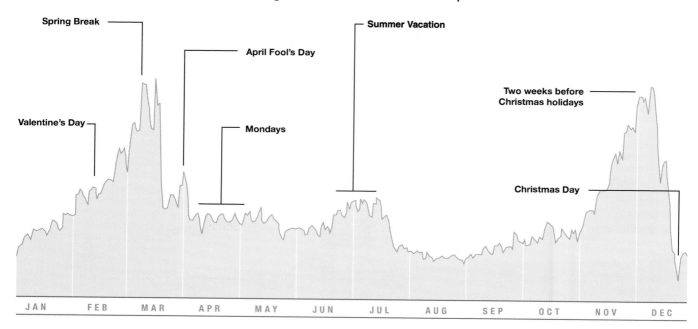

Peak Break-Up Times
According to Facebook status updates

Spring Break

Valentine's Day

April Fool's Day

Mondays

Summer Vacation

Two weeks before Christmas holidays

Christmas Day

JAN FEB MAR APR MAY JUN JUL AUG SEP OCT NOV DEC

PART 1

MINING INFORMATION

PREVIEWING

A. Look at the infographic above. What does *break-up* mean? Why do you think the number of posts about break-ups is higher or lower at certain times of the year? Discuss with a partner.

B. Read this excerpt from the talk. What words do you think are missing? Fill in each blank and share your ideas with a partner.

❝ [Data] is a really fertile medium, and it feels like visualizations, infographics, data

visualizations, they feel like flowers blooming from this medium. But if you _____

at it directly, it's just a lot of _____ and disconnected facts. But if you start working

with it and playing with it in a certain way, interesting things can appear and different

_____ can be revealed. ❞

---

fertile: *adj.* full of possibilities; when used to describe land: able to produce plants

medium: *n.* a way of communicating with people

blooming: *v.* used to describe flowers opening

GETTING THE MAIN IDEA

Watch (▶) the first segment of the talk and check your answers to the Previewing exercises. Then answer the questions below.

1. How did McCandless and Lee Byron collect the data for the infographic on page 144?

    _____

2. What does McCandless do to find interesting things from this "titanic amount of data"?

    _____

CRITICAL THINKING

1. Reflecting. Do you think the infographic tells the whole story about when people might break up with each other? Why or why not? Write your ideas and then discuss with a partner.

    _____

    _____

2. Analyzing. People say "data is the new oil," but McCandless changes it to "data is the new soil." How is data like oil? How is it like soil? Discuss with a partner.

PART 2

INTERACTING WITH DATA

UNDERSTANDING MAIN IDEAS

Read the quote below and choose the statement that best describes what McCandless means.

❝ . . . visualizing information like this is a form of knowledge compression. It's a way of squeezing an enormous amount of information and understanding into a small space. ❞

a. It's difficult to see the connections between different types of data.

b. Infographics let us represent a lot of data in pictures.

c. When you create an infographic, you have to do a lot of research.

UNDERSTANDING KEY DETAILS

A. The statements below are about the "Snake Oil" infographic in McCandless's talk. Watch (▶) the next segment of McCandless's talk and write *T* for True and *F* for False.

_____ **1.** There is less evidence that the supplements at the top are effective.

_____ **2.** McCandless found all of the information for this infographic from one study.

_____ **3.** It takes a long time to update the infographic with new information.

_____ **4.** With the interactive version, you can choose to see only certain supplements.

B. Read this excerpt below from McCandless's talk. Match each bolded word with the correct definition.

❝ [I]nformation design is about solving information problems. It feels like we have a lot of information problems in our society at the moment, from the overload and the saturation to the **breakdown** of trust and **reliability** and runaway **skepticism** and lack of **transparency**, or even just interestingness. I mean, I find information just too interesting. It has a magnetic quality that draws me in. ❞

_____ **1.** breakdown

_____ **2.** reliability

_____ **3.** skepticism

_____ **4.** transparency

a. doubt that something is true

b. ability to be trusted

c. openness

d. a situation in which something is failing

CRITICAL THINKING

1. Interpreting. McCandless says: "Let the dataset change your mindset." Explain this idea in your own words. How does the "Snake Oil" infographic illustrate this idea?

_____

_____

_____

2. Reflecting. In your opinion, which infographic from McCandless's TED Talk is the most effective? Why?

EXPLORE MORE

Watch McCandless's full TED Talk at TED.com. What did you learn from the other infographics he shows? Share your information with the class.

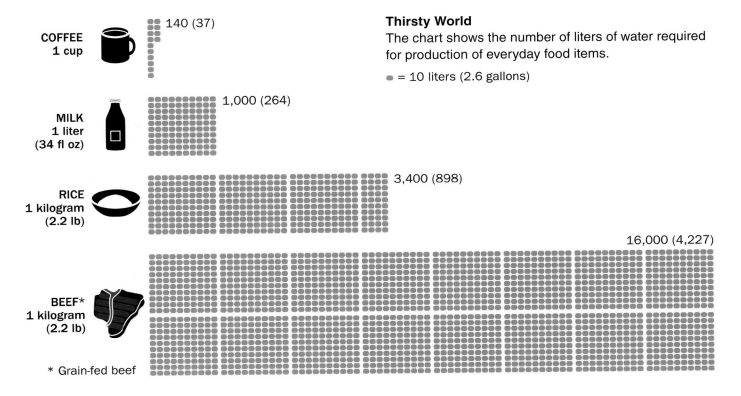

COFFEE
1 cup
140 (37)

MILK
1 liter
(34 fl oz)
1,000 (264)

RICE
1 kilogram
(2.2 lb)
3,400 (898)

BEEF*
1 kilogram
(2.2 lb)
16,000 (4,227)

* Grain-fed beef

Thirsty World
The chart shows the number of liters of water required for production of everyday food items.

= 10 liters (2.6 gallons)

A. **Work with a partner. You are going to research and present an infographic. Follow the steps below:**

1. Find a topic to investigate. You can use one of the topics from this book.

2. Research your topic to find relevant and interesting data.

3. Plan the most important pieces of data you want to show visually. For example, if you have data representing a number of categories, you could present the information as a chart like the one above.

B. **Use the data you collected above to create an infographic. Use the information you learned in this unit about well-designed infographics.**

C. **Use your information to create a short presentation. Use your infographic to explain your information.**

EXPLORE MORE

Watch Aaron Koblin's TED Talk "Visualizing ourselves . . . with crowd-sourced data." Choose one of the infographics Koblin created and explain it to your class.

TEDTALK VIDEO TRANSCRIPTS

DEREK SIVERS:
How to Start a Movement

Part 1

So, ladies and gentlemen, at TED we talk a lot about leadership and how to make a movement. So let's watch a movement happen, start to finish, in under three minutes and dissect some lessons from it.

First, of course you know, a leader needs the guts to stand out and be ridiculed. But what he's doing is so easy to follow. So here's his first follower with a crucial role; he's going to show everyone else how to follow.

Now, notice that the leader embraces him as an equal. So, now it's not about the leader anymore; it's about them, plural. Now, there he is calling to his friends. Now, if you notice that the first follower is actually an underestimated form of leadership in itself. It takes guts to stand out like that. The first follower is what transforms a lone nut into a leader.

And here comes a second follower. Now it's not a lone nut, it's not two nuts—three is a crowd, and a crowd is news. So a movement must be public. It's important to show not just the leader, but the followers, because you find that new followers emulate the followers, not the leader.

Now, here come two more people, and immediately after, three more people. Now we've got momentum. This is the tipping point. Now we've got a movement. So, notice that, as more people join in, it's less risky. So those that were sitting on the fence before, now have no reason not to. They won't stand out, they won't be ridiculed, but they will be part of the in-crowd if they hurry. So, over the next minute, you'll see all of those that prefer to stick with the crowd because eventually they would be ridiculed for not joining in. And that's how you make a movement.

Part 2

But let's recap some lessons from this. So first, if you are the type, like the shirtless dancing guy that is standing alone, remember the importance of nurturing your first few followers as equals so it's clearly about the movement, not you. Okay, but we might have missed the real lesson here.

The biggest lesson, if you noticed—Did you catch it? —is that leadership is over-glorified. That, yes, it was the shirtless guy who was first, and he'll get all the credit, but it was really the first follower that transformed the lone nut into a leader. So, as we're told that we should all be leaders, that would be really ineffective.

If you really care about starting a movement, have the courage to follow and show others how to follow. And when you find a lone nut doing something great, have the guts to be the first one to stand up and join in. And what a perfect place to do that, at TED.

Thanks.

NALINI NADKARNI
Conserving the Canopy

Part 1

. . . I'd like to take you all on a journey up to the forest canopy, and share with you what canopy researchers are asking and also how they're communicating with other people outside of science.

Let's start our journey on the forest floor of one of my study sites in Costa Rica. Because of the overhanging leaves and branches, you'll notice that the understory is very dark, it's very still. And what I'd like to do is take you up to the canopy, not by putting all of you into ropes and harnesses, but rather showing you a very short clip from a National Geographic film called "Heroes of the High Frontier." This was filmed in Monteverde, Costa Rica, and I think it gives us the best impression of what it's like to climb a giant strangler fig. . . .

Up in the canopy, if you were sitting next to me and you turned around from those primary forest ecosystems, you would also see scenes like this. Scenes of forest destruction, forest harvesting, and forest fragmentation, thereby making that intact tapestry of the canopy unable to function in the marvelous ways that it has when it is not disturbed by humans.

I've also looked out on urban places like this and thought about people who are disassociated from trees in their lives. People who grew up in a place like this did not have the opportunity to climb trees and form a relationship with trees and forests, as I did when I was a young girl. This troubles me. . . .

Part 2

In the Pacific Northwest, there's a whole industry of moss-harvesting from old-growth forests. These mosses are taken from the forest; they're used by the floriculture industry, by florists, to make arrangements and make hanging baskets. It's a 265-million-dollar industry, and it's increasing rapidly. . . . [What] has been stripped off of these trunks in the Pacific Northwest old-growth forest is going to take decades and decades to come back. So this whole industry is unsustainable. What can I, as an ecologist, do about that?

Well, my thought was that I could learn how to grow mosses, and that way we wouldn't have to take them out of the wild. And I thought, if I had some partners that could help me with this, that would be great. And so, I thought perhaps incarcerated men and women—who don't have access to nature, who often have a lot of time, they often have space, and you don't need any sharp tools to work with mosses—would be great partners. And they have become excellent partners. The best I can imagine. They were very enthusiastic.

They were incredibly enthusiastic about the work. They learned how to distinguish different species of mosses, which, to tell you the truth, is a lot more than my undergraduate students at the Evergreen College can do. And they embraced the idea that they could help develop a research design in order to grow these mosses. We've been successful as partners in figuring out which species grow the fastest, and I've just been overwhelmed with how successful this has been. Because the prison wardens were very enthusiastic about this as well, I started a science and sustainability seminar in the prisons. I brought my scientific colleagues and sustainability practitioners into the prison. We gave talks once a month, and that actually ended up implementing some amazing sustainability projects at the prisons—organic gardens, worm culture, recycling, water catchment and beekeeping.

. . . Given the duress that we're feeling environmentally in these times, it is time for scientists to reach outward, and time for those outside of science to reach towards academia as well. I started my career with trying to understand the mysteries of forests with the tools of science. By making these partnerships that I described to you, I have really opened my mind and, I have to say, my heart to have a greater understanding, to make other discoveries about nature and myself.

When I look into my heart, I see trees—this is actually an image of a real heart—there are trees in our hearts, there are trees in your hearts. When we come to understand nature, we are touching the most deep, the most important parts of our self. In these partnerships, I have also learned that people tend to compartmentalize themselves into IT people, and movie star people, and scientists, but when we share nature, when we share our perspectives about nature, we find a common denominator. . . .

Thank you very much.

This is an edited version of Nadkarni's 2009 TED Talk. To watch the full talk, visit TED.com.

Unit 3

JANE CHEN

A Warm Embrace that Saves Lives

Part 1

Please close your eyes, and open your hands. Now imagine what you could place in your hands: an apple, maybe your wallet. Now open your eyes. What about a life?

What you see here is a premature baby. He looks like he's resting peacefully, but in fact he's struggling to stay alive because he can't regulate his own body temperature. This baby is so tiny he doesn't have enough fat on his body to stay warm. Sadly, 20 million babies like this are born every year around the world. Four million of these babies die annually.

But the bigger problem is that the ones who do survive grow up with severe, long-term health problems. The reason is because in the first month of a baby's life, its only job is to grow. If it's battling hypothermia, its organs can't develop normally, resulting in a range of health problems from diabetes, to heart disease, to low I.Q. Imagine: Many of these problems could be prevented if these babies were just kept warm.

That is the primary function of an incubator. But traditional incubators require electricity and cost up to $20,000. So, you're not going to find them in rural areas of developing countries. As a result, parents resort to local solutions like tying hot water bottles around their babies' bodies, or placing them under light bulbs like the ones you see here—methods that are both ineffective and unsafe. I've seen this firsthand over and over again.

On one of my first trips to India, I met this young woman, Sevitha, who had just given birth to a tiny premature baby, Rani. She took her baby to the nearest village clinic, and the doctor advised her to take Rani to a city hospital so she could be placed in an incubator. But that hospital was over four hours away, and Sevitha didn't have the means to get there, so her baby died.

Inspired by this story, and dozens of other similar stories like this, my team and I realized what was needed was a local solution, something that could work without electricity, that was simple enough for a mother or a midwife to use, given that the majority of births still take place in the home. We needed something that was portable, something that could be sterilized and reused across multiple babies, and something ultra-low-cost compared to the $20,000 that an incubator in the U.S. costs.

Part 2

So, this is what we came up with. What you see here looks nothing like an incubator. It looks like a small sleeping bag for a baby. You can open it up completely. It's waterproof. There's no seams inside so you can sterilize it very easily. But the magic is in this pouch of wax. This is a phase-change material. It's a wax-like substance with a melting point of human body temperature, 37 degrees Celsius. You can melt this simply using hot water and then when it melts it's able to maintain one constant temperature for four to six hours at a time, after which you simply reheat the pouch. So, you then place it into this little pocket back here, and it creates a warm micro-environment for the baby.

Looks simple, but we've reiterated this dozens of times by going into the field to talk to doctors, moms, and clinicians to ensure that this really meets the needs of the local communities. We plan to launch this product in India in 2010, and the target price point will be $25, less than 0.1 percent of the cost of a traditional incubator.

Over the next five years we hope to save the lives of almost a million babies. But the longer-term social impact is a reduction in population growth. This seems counterintuitive, but turns out that as infant mortality is reduced, population sizes also decrease, because parents don't need to anticipate that their babies are going to die. We hope that the Embrace infant warmer and other simple innovations like this represent a new trend for the future of technology: simple, localized, affordable solutions that have the potential to make huge social impact.

In designing this we followed a few basic principles. We really tried to understand the end user—in this case, people like Sevitha. We tried to understand the root of the problem rather than being biased by what already exists. And then we thought of the most simple solution we could to address this problem. In doing this, I believe we can truly bring technology to the masses. And we can save millions of lives through the simple warmth of an Embrace.

Unit 4

JANE McGONIGAL
Gaming Can Make a Better World

Part 1

. . . This picture pretty much sums up why I think games are so essential to the future survival of the human species. Truly. This is a portrait by a photographer named Phil Toledano. He wanted to capture the emotion of gaming, so he set up a camera in front of gamers while they were playing. And this is a classic gaming emotion. Now, if you're not a gamer, you might miss some of the nuance in this photo. You probably see the sense of urgency, a little bit of fear, but intense concentration, deep, deep focus on tackling a really difficult problem.

. . . Now, unfortunately this is more of the face that we see in everyday life now as we try to tackle urgent problems. This is what I call the "I'm Not Good At Life" face, and this is actually me making it. Can you see? Yes. Good. This is actually me making the "I'm Not Good At Life" face. This is a piece of graffiti in my old neighborhood in Berkeley, California, where I did my PhD on why we're better in games than we are in real life. And this is a problem that a lot of gamers have. We feel that we are not as good in reality as we are in games.

And I don't mean just good as in successful, although that's part of it. We do achieve more in game worlds. But I also mean good as in motivated to do something that matters, inspired to collaborate and to cooperate. And when we're in game worlds I believe that many of us become the best version of ourselves, the most likely to help at a moment's notice, the most likely to stick with a problem as long at it takes, to get up after failure and try again. And in real life, when we face failure, when we confront obstacles, we often don't feel that way. We feel overcome, we feel overwhelmed, we feel anxious, maybe depressed, frustrated, or cynical. We never have those feelings when we're playing games, they just don't exist in games.

. . . Gamers are super-empowered, hopeful individuals. These are people who believe that they are individually capable of changing the world. And the only problem is they believe that they are capable of changing virtual worlds and not the real world. That's the problem that I'm trying to solve.

. . . Now, I know you're asking, "How are we going to solve real world problems in games?" Well, that's what I have devoted my work to over the past few years, at the Institute for the Future. We have this banner in our offices in Palo Alto, and it expresses our view of how we should try to relate to the future. We do not want to try to predict the future. What we want to do is make the future. We want to imagine the best-case scenario outcome, and then we want to empower people to make that outcome a reality. We want to imagine epic wins, and then give people the means to achieve the epic win.

Part 2

I'm just going to very briefly show you three games that I've made that are an attempt to give people the means to create epic wins in their own futures. So, this is *World Without Oil*. We made this game in 2007. This is an online game in which you try to survive an oil shortage. The oil shortage is fictional, but we put enough online content out there for you to believe that it's real, and to live your real life as if we've run out of oil. So when you come to the game, you sign up, you tell us where you live, and then we give you real-time news, videos, data feeds that show you exactly how much oil costs, what's not available, how food supply is being affected, how transportation is being affected, if schools are closed, if there is rioting, and you have to figure out how you would live your real life as if this were true. And then we ask you to blog about it, to post videos, to post photos.

We piloted this game with 1,700 players in 2007, and we've tracked them for the three years since. And I can tell you that this is a transformative experience. Nobody wants to change how they live just because it's good for the world, or because we're supposed to. But if you immerse them in an epic adventure and tell them, "We've run out of oil. This is an amazing story and adventure for you to go on. Challenge yourself to see how you would survive," most of our players have kept up the habits that they learned in this game.

So, for the next world-saving game, we decided to aim higher: bigger problem than just peak oil. We did a game called *Superstruct* at the Institute for the Future. And the premise was a supercomputer has calculated that humans have only 23 years left on the planet. This supercomputer was called the Global Extinction Awareness System, of course. We asked people to come online almost like a Jerry Bruckheimer movie. You know Jerry Bruckheimer movies, you form a dream team—you've got the astronaut, the scientist, the ex-convict, and they all have something to do to save the world.

But in our game, instead of just having five people on the dream team, we said, "Everybody's on the dream team, and it's your job to invent the future of energy, the future of food, the future of health, the future of security, and the future of the social safety net." We had 8,000 people play that game for eight weeks. They came up with 500 insanely creative solutions that you can go online, if you Google *Superstruct*, and see.

So, finally, the last game, we're launching it March third. This is a game done with the World Bank Institute. If you complete the game you will be certified by the World Bank Institute as a Social Innovator, class of 2010. Working with universities all over sub-Saharan Africa, and we are inviting them to learn social innovation skills. We've got a graphic novel, we've got leveling-up in skills like local insight, knowledge networking, sustainability, vision, and resourcefulness. I would like to invite all of you to please share this game with young people, anywhere in the world, particularly in developing areas, who might benefit from coming together to try to start to imagine their own social enterprises to save the world.

So, I'm going to wrap up now. I want to ask a question. What do you think happens next? We've got all these amazing gamers, we've got these games that are kind of pilots of what we might do, but none of them have saved the real world yet. Well, I hope that you will agree with me that gamers are a human resource that we can use to do real-world work, that games are a powerful platform for change. We have all these amazing superpowers: blissful productivity, the ability to weave a tight social fabric, this feeling of urgent optimism, and the desire for epic meaning.

I really hope that we can come together to play games that matter, to survive on this planet for another century. And that's my hope, that you will join me in making and playing games like this. When I look forward to the next decade, I know two things for sure: that we can make any future we can imagine, and we can play any games we want. So, I say: Let the world-changing games begin. Thank you.

This is an edited version of McGonigal's 2010 TED Talk. To watch the full talk, visit TED.com.

Unit 5

ANGELA LEE DUCKWORTH
The Key to Success? Grit

Part 1

When I was 27 years old, I left a very demanding job in management consulting for a job that was even more demanding: teaching. I went to teach seventh graders math in the New York City public schools. And like any teacher, I made quizzes and tests. I gave out homework assignments. When the work came back, I calculated grades.

What struck me was that I.Q. was not the only difference between my best and my worst students. Some of my strongest performers did not have stratospheric I.Q. scores. Some of my smartest kids weren't doing so well.

And that got me thinking. The kinds of things you need to learn in seventh grade math, sure, they're hard: ratios, decimals, the area of a parallelogram. But these concepts are not impossible, and I was firmly convinced that every one of my students could learn the material if they worked hard and long enough.

After several more years of teaching, I came to the conclusion that what we need in education is a much better understanding of students and learning from a motivational perspective, from a psychological perspective. In education, the one thing we know how to measure best is I.Q., but what if doing well in school and in life depends on much more than your ability to learn quickly and easily?

Part 2

So I left the classroom, and I went to graduate school to become a psychologist. I started studying kids and adults in all kinds of super challenging settings, and in every study my question was, who is successful here and why? In all those very different contexts, one characteristic emerged as a significant predictor of success. And it wasn't social intelligence. It wasn't good looks, physical health, and it wasn't I.Q. It was grit.

Grit is passion and perseverance for very long-term goals. Grit is having stamina. Grit is sticking with your future, day in, day out, not just for the week, not just for the month, but for years, and working really hard to make that future a reality. Grit is living life like it's a marathon, not a sprint. . . .

Every day, parents and teachers ask me, "How do I build grit in kids? What do I do to teach kids a solid work ethic?

How do I keep them motivated for the long run?" The honest answer is, I don't know. What I do know is that talent doesn't make you gritty. Our data show very clearly that there are many talented individuals who simply do not follow through on their commitments. In fact, in our data, grit is usually unrelated or even inversely related to measures of talent.

So far, the best idea I've heard about building grit in kids is something called "growth mindset." This is an idea developed at Stanford University by Carol Dweck, and it is the belief that the ability to learn is not fixed, that it can change with your effort. Dr. Dweck has shown that when kids read and learn about the brain and how it changes and grows in response to challenge, they're much more likely to persevere when they fail, because they don't believe that failure is a permanent condition.

So growth mindset is a great idea for building grit. But we need more. And that's where I'm going to end my remarks, because that's where we are. That's the work that stands before us. We need to take our best ideas, our strongest intuitions, and we need to test them. We need to measure whether we've been successful, and we have to be willing to fail, to be wrong, to start over again with lessons learned.

In other words, we need to be gritty about getting our kids grittier.

Thank you.

This is an edited version of Duckworth's 2013 TED Talk. To watch the full talk, visit TED.com.

Unit 6

JAMIE OLIVER
Teach Every Child About Food

Part 1

. . . OK, school. What is school? Who invented it? What's the purpose of school? School was always invented to arm us with the tools to make us creative, do wonderful things, make us earn a living, etc., etc., etc. You know, it's been kind of in this sort of tight box for a long, long time. OK? But we haven't really evolved it to deal with the health catastrophes of America, OK? School food is something that most kids—31 million a day, actually—have twice a day, more than often, breakfast and lunch, 180 days of the year. So you could say that school food is quite important, really, judging the circumstances. . . .

Now, the reality is, the food that your kids get every day is fast food, it's highly processed, there's not enough fresh food in there at all. You know, the amount of additives, E numbers, ingredients you wouldn't believe—there's not enough veggies at

all. French fries are considered a vegetable. Pizza for breakfast. They don't even get given crockery. Knives and forks? No, they're too dangerous. They have scissors in the classroom, but knives and forks? No. And the way I look at it is: If you don't have knives and forks in your school, you're purely endorsing, from a state level, fast food, because it's handheld. And yes, by the way, it is fast food: It's sloppy joes, it's burgers, it's wieners, it's pizzas, it's all of that stuff. Ten percent of what we spend on healthcare, as I said earlier, is on obesity, and it's going to double. We're not teaching our kids. There's no statutory right to teach kids about food, elementary or secondary school. OK? We don't teach kids about food. Right? And this is a little clip from an elementary school, which is very common in England.

[Video] *Jamie Oliver: Who knows what this is?*
Child: Potatoes.
JO: Potato? So, you think these are potatoes? Do you know what that is? Do you know what that is?
Child: Broccoli?
JO: What about this? Our good old friend. Do you know what this is, honey?
Child: Celery.
JO: No. What do you think this is?
Child: Onion.
JO: Onion? No.

JO: Immediately you get a really clear sense of: Do the kids know anything about where food comes from?

JO: Who knows what that is?
Child: Uh, pear?
JO: What do you think this is?
Child: I don't know.

JO: If the kids don't know what stuff is, then they will never eat it.

Normal. England and America, England and America. Guess what fixed that. Guess what fixed that: Two one-hour sessions. We've got to start teaching our kids about food in schools, period.

Part 2

I want to tell you about something that kind of epitomizes the trouble that we're in, guys. OK? I want to talk about something so basic as milk. Every kid has the right to milk at school. Your kids will be having milk at school, breakfast and lunch. Right? They'll be having two bottles. OK? And most kids do. But milk ain't good enough anymore. Because someone at the milk board, right—and don't get me wrong, I support milk—but someone at the milk board probably paid a lot of money for some geezer to work out that if you put loads of flavorings and colorings and sugar in milk, right, more kids will drink it. Yeah. . . .

For me, there ain't no need to flavor the milk. Okay? There's sugar in everything. I know the ins and outs of those ingredients. It's in everything. Even the milk hasn't escaped the kind of modern-day problems. There's our milk. There's our carton. In that is nearly as much sugar as one of your favorite cans of fizzy pop, and they are having two a day. So, let me just show you. We've got one kid, here, having, you know, eight tablespoons of sugar a day. You know, there's your week. There's your month. And I've taken the liberty of putting in just the five years of elementary school sugar, just from milk. . . .

Part 3

Obviously in schools we owe it to them to make sure those 180 days of the year, from that little precious age of four, til 18, 20, 24, whatever, they need to be cooked proper, fresh food from local growers on site. OK? There needs to be a new standard of fresh, proper food for your children. Yeah?

Under the circumstances, it's profoundly important that every single American child leaves school knowing how to cook 10 recipes that will save their life. Life skills.

That means that they can be students, young parents, and be able to sort of duck and dive around the basics of cooking, no matter what recession hits them next time. If you can cook, recession money doesn't matter. If you can cook, time doesn't matter. . . .

I know it's weird having an English person standing here before you talking about all this. All I can say is: I care. I'm a father, and I love this country, and I believe truly, actually, that if change can be made in this country, beautiful things will happen around the world. If America does it, I believe other people will follow. It's incredibly important.

When I was in Huntington, trying to get a few things to work when they weren't, I thought "If I had a magic wand, what would I do?" And I thought, "You know what? I'd just love to be put in front of some of the most amazing movers and shakers in America." And a month later, TED phoned me up and gave me this award. I'm here. So, my wish. Dyslexic, so I'm a bit slow. My wish is for you to help a strong, sustainable movement to educate every child about food, to inspire families to cook again, and to empower people everywhere to fight obesity.

Thank you.

This is an edited version of Oliver's 2010 TED Talk. To watch the full talk, visit TED.com.

Unit 7

AMY CUDDY
Your Body Language Shapes Who You Are

Part 1

. . . So we're really fascinated with body language, and we're particularly interested in other people's body language. You know, we're interested in, like, you know, an awkward interaction, or a smile, or a contemptuous glance, or maybe a very awkward wink, . . .

So social scientists have spent a lot of time looking at the effects of our body language, or other people's body language, on judgments. And we make sweeping judgments and inferences from body language. And those judgments can predict really meaningful life outcomes, like who we hire or promote, who we ask out on a date. . . .

So when we think of nonverbals, we think of how we judge others, how they judge us, and what the outcomes are. We tend to forget, though, the other audience that's influenced by our nonverbals, and that's ourselves. . . .

Part 2

So my main collaborator Dana Carney, who's at Berkeley, and I really wanted to know, can you fake it till you make it? Like, can you do this just for a little while and actually experience a behavioral outcome that makes you seem more powerful? So we know that our nonverbals govern how other people think and feel about us. There's a lot of evidence. But our question really was, do our nonverbals govern how we think and feel about ourselves?. . .

So this is what we did. We decided to bring people into the lab and run a little experiment, and these people adopted, for two minutes, either high-power poses or low-power poses, and I'm just going to show you five of the poses, although they took on only two. So here's one. A couple more. This one has been dubbed the "Wonder Woman" by the media. Here are a couple more. So you can be standing or you can be sitting. And here are the low-power poses. So you're folding up, you're making yourself small. This one is very low-power. When you're touching your neck, you're really protecting yourself. So this is what happens. They come in, they spit into a vial, we for two minutes say, "You need to do this or this." They don't look at pictures of the poses. We don't want to prime them with a concept of power. We want them to be feeling power, right? So two minutes they do this. We then ask them, "How powerful do you feel?" on a series of items, and then we give them an opportunity to gamble, and then we take another saliva sample. That's it. That's the whole experiment.

So this is what we find. Risk tolerance, which is the gambling, what we find is that when you're in the high-power pose condition, 86 percent of you will gamble. When you're in the low-power pose condition, only 60 percent, and that's a pretty whopping significant difference.

Here's what we find on testosterone. From their baseline when they come in, high-power people experience about a 20-percent increase, and low-power people experience about a 10-percent decrease. So again, two minutes, and you get these changes. Here's what you get on cortisol. High-power people experience about a 25-percent decrease, and the low-power people experience about a 15-percent increase.

So two minutes lead to these hormonal changes that configure your brain to basically be either assertive, confident, and comfortable, or really stress-reactive, and, you know, feeling sort of shut down. And we've all had the feeling, right? So it seems that our nonverbals do govern how we think and feel about ourselves, so it's not just others, but it's also ourselves. Also, our bodies change our minds.

Part 3

. . . So when I tell people about this, that our bodies change our minds and our minds can change our behavior, and our behavior can change our outcomes, they say to me, "I don't— It feels fake." Right? So I said, "fake it till you make it." "I don't—It's not me. I don't want to get there and then still feel like a fraud. I don't want to feel like an impostor. I don't want to get there only to feel like I'm not supposed to be here." And that really resonated with me, because I want to tell you a little story about being an impostor and feeling like I'm not supposed to be here.

When I was 19, I was in a really bad car accident. I was thrown out of a car, rolled several times. I was thrown from the car. And I woke up in a head injury rehab ward, and I had been withdrawn from college, and I learned that my I.Q. had dropped by two standard deviations, which was very traumatic.

I knew my I.Q. because I had identified with being smart, and I had been called gifted as a child. So I'm taken out of college, I keep trying to go back. They say, "You're not going to finish college. Just, you know, there are other things for you to do, but that's not going to work out for you." So I really struggled with this, and I have to say, having your identity taken from you, your core identity, and for me it was being smart, having that taken from you, there's nothing that leaves you feeling more powerless than that. So I felt entirely powerless. I worked and worked and worked, and I got lucky, and worked, and got lucky, and worked.

Eventually I graduated from college. It took me four years longer than my peers, and I convinced someone, my angel advisor, Susan Fiske, to take me on, and so I ended up at Princeton, and I was like, I am not supposed to be here. I am an impostor. And the night before my first-year talk, and the first-year talk at Princeton is a 20-minute talk to 20 people. That's it. I was so afraid of being found out the next day that I called her and said, "I'm quitting." She was like, "You are not quitting, because I took a gamble on you, and you're staying. You're going to stay, and this is what you're going to do. You are going to fake it. You're going to do every talk that you ever get asked to do. You're just going to do it and do it and do it, even if you're terrified and just paralyzed and having an out-of-body experience, until you have this moment where you say, 'Oh my gosh, I'm doing it. Like, I have become this. I am actually doing this.'" So that's what I did. . . .

So at the end of my first year at Harvard, a student who had not talked in class the entire semester, who I had said, "Look, you've gotta participate or else you're going to fail," came into my office. I really didn't know her at all. And she said, she came in totally defeated, and she said, "I'm not supposed to be here." And that was the moment for me. Because two things happened. One was that I realized, oh my gosh, I don't feel like that anymore. You know. I don't feel that anymore, but she does, and I get that feeling. And the second was, she is supposed to be here! Like, she can fake it, she can become it. So I was like, "Yes, you are! You are supposed to be here! And tomorrow you're going to fake it, you're going to make yourself powerful, and, you know, you're gonna—" "And you're going to go into the classroom, and you are going to give the best comment ever." You know? And she gave the best comment ever, and people turned around and they were like, oh my God, I didn't even notice her sitting there, you know?

She comes back to me months later, and I realized that she had not just faked it till she made it, she had actually faked it till she became it. So she had changed. And so I want to say to you, don't fake it till you make it. Fake it till you become it. . . .

So I want to ask you first, you know, both to try power posing, and also I want to ask you to share the science, because this is simple. I don't have ego involved in this. Give it away. Share it with people, because the people who can use it the most are the ones with no resources and no technology and no status and no power. Give it to them because they can do it in private. They need their bodies, privacy and two minutes, and it can significantly change the outcomes of their life.

Thank you.

This is an edited version of Cuddy's 2012 TED Talk. To watch the full talk, visit TED.com.

Unit 8

WILLIAM KAMKWAMBA

How I Harnessed the Wind

Part 1

Thank you. Two years ago, I stood on the TED stage in Arusha, Tanzania. I spoke very briefly about one of my proudest creations. It was a simple machine that changed my life.

Before that time, I had never been away from my home in Malawi. I had never used a computer. I had never seen an Internet. On the stage that day, I was so nervous. My English lost, I wanted to vomit. I had never been surrounded by so many *azungu*, white people.

There was a story I wouldn't tell you then. But well, I'm feeling good right now. I would like to share that story today. We have seven children in my family. All sisters, excepting me. This is me with my dad when I was a little boy. Before I discovered the wonders of science, I was just a simple farmer in a country of poor farmers. Like everyone else, we grew maize.

One year, our fortune turned very bad. In 2001 we experienced an awful famine. Within five months all Malawians began to starve to death. My family ate one meal per day, at night. Only three swallows of nsima for each one of us. The food passes through our bodies. We drop down to nothing.

In Malawi, the secondary school, you have to pay school fees. Because of the hunger, I was forced to drop out of school. I looked at my father and looked at those dry fields. It was the future I couldn't accept.

I felt very happy to be at the secondary school, so I was determined to do anything possible to receive education. So I went to a library. I read books, science books, especially physics. I couldn't read English that well. I used diagrams and pictures to learn the words around them.

Part 2

Another book put that knowledge in my hands. It said a windmill could pump water and generate electricity. Pump water meant irrigation, a defense against hunger, which we were experiencing by that time. So I decided I would build one windmill for myself. But I didn't have materials to use, so I went to a scrap yard where I found my materials. Many people, including my mother, said I was crazy.

I found a tractor fan, shock absorber, PVC pipes. Using a bicycle frame and an old bicycle dynamo, I built my machine. It was one light at first. And then four lights, with switches, and even a circuit breaker, modeled after an electric bell. Another machine pumps water for irrigation.

Queues of people start lining up at my house to charge their mobile phone. I could not get rid of them. And the reporters came too, which lead to bloggers and which lead to a call from something called TED. I had never seen an airplane before. I had never slept in a hotel. So, on stage that day in Arusha, my English lost, I said something like, "I tried. And I made it."

So I would like to say something to all the people out there like me to the Africans, and the poor who are struggling with your dreams. God bless. Maybe one day you will watch this on the Internet. I say to you, trust yourself and believe. Whatever happens, don't give up. Thank you.

Unit 9

SUE AUSTIN

Deep Sea Diving . . . In a Wheelchair

Part 1

. . . I started using a wheelchair 16 years ago when an extended illness changed the way I could access the world. When I started using the wheelchair, it was a tremendous new freedom. I'd seen my life slip away and become restricted. It was like having an enormous new toy. I could whiz around and feel the wind in my face again. Just being out on the street was exhilarating.

But even though I had this newfound joy and freedom, people's reaction completely changed towards me. It was as if they couldn't see me anymore, as if an invisibility cloak had descended. They seemed to see me in terms of their assumptions of what it must be like to be in a wheelchair. When I asked people their associations with the wheelchair, they used words like *limitation, fear, pity,* and *restriction*. I realized I'd internalized these responses and it had changed who I was on a core level. A part of me had become alienated from myself. I was seeing myself not from my perspective, but vividly and continuously from the perspective of other people's responses to me.

As a result, I knew I needed to make my own stories about this experience, new narratives to reclaim my identity.

Part 2

I started making work that aimed to communicate something of the joy and freedom I felt when using a wheelchair—a power chair—to negotiate the world. I was working to transform these internalized responses, to transform the preconceptions that had so shaped my identity when I started using a wheelchair, by creating unexpected images. The wheelchair became an object to paint and play with. When I literally started leaving traces of my joy and freedom, it was exciting to see the interested and surprised responses from people. It seemed to open up new perspectives, and therein lay the paradigm shift. It showed that an arts practice can remake one's identity and transform preconceptions by revisioning the familiar.

So when I began to dive, in 2005, I realized scuba gear extends your range of activity in just the same way as a wheelchair does, but the associations attached to scuba gear are ones of excitement and adventure, completely different to people's responses to the wheelchair.

So I thought, "I wonder what'll happen if I put the two together?" [Laughter] And the underwater wheelchair that has resulted has taken me on the most amazing journey over the last seven years.

So to give you an idea of what that's like, I'd like to share with you one of the outcomes from creating this spectacle, and show you what an amazing journey it's taken me on. . . .

It is the most amazing experience, beyond most other things I've experienced in life. I literally have the freedom to move in 360 degrees of space and an ecstatic experience of joy and freedom.

And the incredibly unexpected thing is that other people seem to see and feel that too. Their eyes literally light up, and they say things like, "I want one of those," or, "If you can do that, I can do anything."

And I'm thinking, it's because in that moment of them seeing an object they have no frame of reference for, or so transcends the frames of reference they have with the wheelchair, they have to think in a completely new way. And I think that moment of completely new thought perhaps creates a freedom that spreads to the rest of other people's lives. For me, this means that they're seeing the value of difference, the joy it brings when instead of focusing on loss or limitation, we see and discover the power and joy of seeing the world from exciting new perspectives. For me, the wheelchair becomes a vehicle for transformation. In fact, I now call the underwater wheelchair "Portal," because it's literally pushed me through into a new way of being, into new dimensions and into a new level of consciousness.

And the other thing is, that because nobody's seen or heard of an underwater wheelchair before, and creating this spectacle is about creating new ways of seeing, being and knowing, now you have this concept in your mind. You're all part of the artwork too.

This is an edited version of Austin's 2012 TED Talk.
To watch the full talk, visit TED.com.

DAVID McCANDLESS
The Beauty of Data Visualization

Part 1

. . . So, I've been working as a data journalist for about a year, and I keep hearing a phrase all the time, which is this: "Data is the new oil." Data is the kind of ubiquitous resource that we can shape to provide new innovations and new insights, and it's all around us, and it can be mined very easily. It's not a particularly great metaphor in these times, especially if you live around the Gulf of Mexico, but I would, perhaps, adapt this metaphor slightly, and I would say that data is the new soil. Because for me, it feels like a fertile, creative medium. Over the years, online, we've laid down a huge amount of information and data, and we irrigate it with networks and connectivity, and it's been worked and tilled by unpaid workers and governments. And, all right, I'm kind of milking the metaphor a little bit. But it's a really fertile medium, and it feels like visualizations, infographics, data visualizations, they feel like flowers blooming from this medium. But if you look at it directly, it's just a lot of numbers and disconnected facts. But if you start working with it and playing with it in a certain way, interesting things can appear and different patterns can be revealed.

Let me show you this. Can you guess what this data set is? What rises twice a year, once in Easter and then two weeks before Christmas, has a mini peak every Monday, and then flattens out over the summer? I'll take answers. [Audience: Chocolate.] David McCandless: Chocolate. You might want to get some chocolate in. Any other guesses? [Audience: Shopping.] DM: Shopping. Yeah, retail therapy might help. [Audience: Sick leave.] DM: Sick leave. Yeah, you'll definitely want to take some time off. Shall we see?

So, the information guru Lee Byron and myself, we scraped 10,000 status Facebook updates for the phrase "break-up" and "broken-up" and this is the pattern we found —people clearing out for Spring Break, [Laughter] coming out of very bad weekends on a Monday, being single over the summer, and then the lowest day of the year, of course: Christmas Day. Who would do that? So there's a titanic amount of data out there now, unprecedented. But if you ask the right kind of question, or you work it in the right kind of way, interesting things can emerge. . . .

Part 2

We need relative figures that are connected to other data so that we can see a fuller picture, and then that can lead to us changing our perspective. As Hans Rosling, the master, my master, said, "Let the dataset change your mindset." And if it can do that, maybe it can also change your behavior.

Take a look at this one. I'm a bit of a health nut. I love taking supplements and being fit, but I can never understand what's going on in terms of evidence. There's always conflicting evidence. Should I take vitamin C? Should I be taking wheatgrass? This is a visualization of all the evidence for nutritional supplements. This kind of diagram is called a balloon race. So the higher up the image, the more evidence there is for each supplement. And the bubbles correspond to popularity as regards to Google hits. So you can immediately apprehend the relationship between efficacy and popularity, but you can also, if you grade the evidence, do a "worth it" line. So supplements above this line are worth investigating, but only for the conditions listed below, and then the supplements below the line are perhaps not worth investigating.

Now this image constitutes a huge amount of work. We scraped like 1,000 studies from PubMed, the biomedical database, and we compiled them and graded them all. And it was incredibly frustrating for me because I had a book of 250 visualizations to do for my book, and I spent a month doing this, and I only filled two pages. But what it points to is that visualizing information like this is a form of knowledge compression. It's a way of squeezing an enormous amount of information and understanding into a small space. And once you've curated that data, and once you've cleaned that data, and once it's there, you can do cool stuff like this.

So I converted this into an interactive app, so I can now generate this application online—this is the visualization online—and I can say, "Yeah, brilliant." So it spawns itself. And then I can say, "Well, just show me the stuff that affects heart health." So let's filter that out. So heart is filtered out, so I can see if I'm curious about that. I think, "No, no. I don't want to take any synthetics, I just want to see plants and—just show me herbs and plants. I've got all the natural ingredients." Now this app is spawning itself from the data. The data is all stored in a Google Doc, and it's literally generating itself from that data. So the data is now alive; this is a living image, and I can update it in a second. New evidence comes out. I just change a row on a spreadsheet. Doosh! Again, the image recreates itself. So it's cool. It's kind of living. . . .

So, just to wrap up, I wanted to say that it feels to me that design is about solving problems and providing elegant solutions, and information design is about solving information problems. And it feels like we have a lot of information problems in our society at the moment, from the overload and the saturation to the breakdown of trust and reliability and runaway skepticism and lack of transparency, or even just interestingness. I mean, I find information just too interesting. It has a magnetic quality that draws me in. . . .

This is an edited version of McCandless's 2010 TED Talk. To watch the full talk, visit TED.com.

VOCABULARY LOG

As you complete each unit, use this chart to record definitions and example sentences of key vocabulary. Add other useful words or phrases you learn.

Unit	Vocabulary	Definition/Example
1	attract	
	feature*	
	focus*	
	in other words	
	leadership	
	purpose	
	show up	
	stand out	
	_____	
2	attach*	
	capacity*	
	damage	
	innovative	
	layer	
	mysterious	
	survive*	
	sustainable*	
	_____	
3	adjust*	
	affordable	
	available*	
	device*	
	estimate*	
	plentiful	
	portable	
	temporary*	
	_____	
4	accomplishment	
	characteristic	
	cooperation*	
	form	
	involve*	
	predict	
	resource*	
	significant*	
	_____	
5	approach*	
	coach	
	combine	
	determined	
	engaged	
	indicate*	
	promising	
	relevant*	
	_____	

Unit	Vocabulary	Definition/Example
6	awareness*	
	consumer*	
	nutrition	
	participate*	
	replace	
	revolution*	
	urge	
	widespread*	
7	confident	
	conversely*	
	cope	
	favorably	
	prove	
	qualification	
	release*	
	stress*	
8	altitude	
	consistent*	
	generate*	
	practical	
	source*	
	surface	
	traditional	
	visible*	
9	affect*	
	arrange	
	ignore*	
	severe	
	simulation*	
	specific*	
	visually*	
	welfare*	
10	appreciate*	
	complex*	
	connection	
	consume*	
	create*	
	enhance*	
	magical*	
	visualize*	

* These words are on the Academic Word List (AWL), a list of the 570 most frequent word families in academic texts. The AWL does not include words that are among the most frequent 2,000 words of English. For more information, see www.victoria.ac.nz/lals/resources/academicwordlist/

Photo, Map and Infographic Credits

8-9 © AFP/Getty Images, **10-11** © Francis Miller/Getty Images, **12**(b) © AP Images/Rob Croese, **13**(t) ©Tyrone siu/Reuters, **16-17** © James Duncan Davidson/TED, **21**(t) © Time Life Pictures/Getty Images, **22-23** © Rob Nelson, **24-25** © Jon Huey/The Evergreen State College, **26**(c)(b) © FRANS LANTING/National Geographic Creative, **26**(b) © National Geographic, **27**(t) ©TIM LAMAN/National Geographic Creative, **27**(br) © DAVID LIITTSCHWAGER/National Geographic Creative, **29**(tr) © Jason Edwards/National Geographic Creative, **30-31** © James Duncan Davidson/TED, **32**(b) © JAMES P. BLAIR/National Geographic Creative, **35**(t) © Benj Drummond, **36-37** © Ami Vitale/Ripple Effect Images, **39**(tl)(tr)(cl)(cr) © Michael Lewis, **40**(c)(bl)(br) © Reaction Housing, **41**(t) © Reaction Housing, **44-45** © Marla Aufmuth, **48**(t) © Alejandra Villalobos/Embrace Global, **48**(b) © Embrace Global, **49**(t) © Vestergaard Frandsen, **50-51** © FREDERIC J. BROWN/Getty Images, **52-53** © World of Warcraft, **55**(t) © James Duncan Davidson/TED, **58-59** © James Duncan Davidson, **61**(c) © World Without Oil, **61**(bc) © Superstruct, **63**(t) © Urgent Evoke/World Bank/Jacob Glaser, **64-65** © James P. Blair/National Geographic Creative, **66-67** © Tyrone Turner/National Geographic Creative, **68**(bl) © Noka Studio/Shutterstock.com, **68**(br) © Hundvene-Clements Photography/Scott Brownrigg/The Da Vinci Studio School, **69**(t) © Mike Theiss/National Geographic Creative, **72-73** © Ryan Lash/TED, **77** © Christopher Herwig/Aurora Photos, **78-79** © Edwin Remsberg/VWPics/Redux,, **80-81** © Brian Finke/National Geographic Creative, **83**(t) © Mitch Haddad/ABC via Getty Images, **86-87** © James Duncan Davidson, **88**(tl) © Maks Narodenko/Shutterstock.com, **88**(tr) ©Lithian/Shutterstock.com, **88**(cl) © Dmitrij Skorobogatov/Shutterstock.com, **88**(cr) © Danny Smythe/Shutterstock, **88**(cl) ©n7atal7i/Shutterstock.com, **88**(cr) © Nattika/Shutterstock.com, **89**(b) © Marla Aufmuth, **91**(t) ©Tristan Fewings/Getty Images/Entertainment/Getty Images, **92-93** © Richard Heathcote/Getty Images, Sport/Getty Images, **94-95** ©Julian Finney/Getty Images/Sport/Getty Images, **96**(c) © TED, **97**(t) © Alex Saberi/National Geographic Creative, **100-101** © James Duncan Davidson/TED, **105**(tl)(tr) © Dailey Crafton/Lockstep Studio, **106-107** © Paul Richman/500px Prime, **108-109** © Andrea Dunlap/Makani/GoogleX, **111**(t) © Sarah Leen/National Geographic Creative, **113**(b) © Andrea Dunlap/Makani/GoogleX, **115** © William Kamkwamba/TED, **117**(b) © Lucas Oleniuk/Toronto Star/Getty Images, **119**(t) © Deanne Fitzmaurice/National Geographic Creative, **120-121** © RED/Freewheeling/Norman Lomax, **122-123** © Rosalie Winard, **124**(b) © CharitySub, **125**(t) © Temple Grandin, **128-129** © Lloyd Russell, **130**(t) © Richard Jeffery, **132**(b) © Lloyd Russell, **133**(t) Zhou Ge/Xinhua Press/Corbis Wire/Corbis, **134-135** © John Tomanio, NGM Staff. Cartogram: XNR Productions and John Tomanio. Sources: World Bank, CIA World Fact Book, Econstats (Cartogram); UN (Population Graphic); Oxford Forecasting (GDP Graphic); U.S. Energy Information Agency (Energy Graphic; OECD is the Organization for Economic Cooperation and Development), **136-137, 138, 141** David McCandless, InformationisBeautiful.net, **143** © James Duncan Davidson/TED, **144, 147** Source: Hoekstra, A.Y./Chapagain, A.K. 2008

Acknowledgements

The Authors and Publisher would like to thank the following teaching professionals for their valuable input during the development of this series:

Coleeta Paradise Abdullah, Certified Training Center; **Wilder Yesid Escobar Almeciga,** Universidad El Bosque; **Tara Amelia Arntsen,** Northern State University; **Mei-ho Chiu,** Soochow University; **Amy Cook,** Bowling Green State University; **Anthony Sean D'Amico,** SDH Institute; **Mariel Doyenart,** Alianza Cultural Uruguay-Estados Unidos; **Raichle Farrelly,** American University of Armenia; **Douglas E. Forster,** Japan Women's University; **Rosario Giraldez,** Alianza Cultural Uruguay-Estados Unidos; **Floyd H. Graham III,** Kansai Gaidai University; **Jay Klaphake,** Kyoto University of Foreign Studies; **Anthony G. Lavigne,** Kansai Gaidai University; **Adriana Castañeda Londoño,** Centro Colombo Americano; **Alexandra Dylan Lowe,** SUNY Westchester Community College; **Elizabeth Ortiz Lozada,** COPEI - COPOL English Institute; **David Matijasevich,** Canadian Education College; **Jennie Popp,** Universidad Andrés Bello; **Ubon Pun-ubon,** Sripatum University; **Yoko Sakurai,** Aichi University; **Michael J. Sexton,** PSB Academy; **Jenay Seymour,** Hongik University; **Karenne Sylvester,** New College Manchester; **Mark S. Turnoy; Hajime Uematsu,** Hirosaki University; **Nae-Dong Yang,** National Taiwan University;

And special thanks to: Nalini Nadkarni, Jane Chen, David McCandless, Temple Grandin, Reaction Housing, Inc., Embrace Global, Makani by Google [x] World Bank, Da Vinci Studio School